The 770 Account

How to Fund Your Own ***Worry-Free,*** ***100% Tax-Free*** *Retirement*

Tom Dyson

Palm Beach Research Group

What Some of Our Readers Are Saying About the 770 Account

"I have used the 770 Account strategy for three years now. The one thing I can tell everyone is: It provides freedom! I love using it. I loved it so much that I personally became licensed to sell it.

"I personally have two of these accounts and have taken over all of my debt with them in only two years. Being able to live, save, invest, and get out of debt all at the same time with one financial product is a freedom."—Wade B.

"I started two of these accounts before you even published info about this unbelievable wealth-building product... My only regret is I did not learn about this product in my 20s. What a mistake! Very smart of you to bring this to the attention of your members. Nice job!"—Kevin O.

"Just wanted to let you at *The Palm Beach Letter* know that you are on the right track with the 770 Account. I set up a 770 Account several years ago and immediately understood the power of this program...

"There are so many benefits with a 770 Account. It's only limited to one's imagination. What's important to understand is that this program works. It requires some discipline, but everyone who tries this will be happy with it. I no longer have to deal with the bank for a loan. And after three years of doing this, I don't really stress over finances anymore."—Robert C.

"Your 770 Account research has really hit home for me. Keep up the great work. You have given me plenty of food for thought. Because of your persuasive case, I will probably start an account for my wife and daughter as well."—Bobby J.

"This is a great resource. I've opened two accounts with your encouragement!"—Don P.

"I appreciate Tom's enthusiasm for the 770 Account. About 10 years ago, I was lucky enough to learn about this. One of the reasons it's not so widespread is that it's not sexy, it's not immediate, and it requires some fiscal discipline over time."—James F.

"In my case, I have turned 66, am semiretired, and am looking at pulling my 401(k) apart and moving it into a 770 Account. After paying the taxes to Uncle Sam, I can safely with peace of mind make money on my new savings account."—Paul M.

The 770 Account

*How to Fund Your Own **Worry-Free**, **100% Tax-Free** Retirement*

Tom Dyson

Palm Beach Research Group

ISBN 978-0-9963632-0-4

Published by:
The Palm Beach Research Group
Delray Beach, Florida

www.palmbeachgroup.com

Edited by:
Tim Mittelstaedt

PALM BEACH RESEARCH GROUP

About the Palm Beach Research Group

The Palm Beach Research Group is an independent financial publishing company based in Delray Beach, Florida. It publishes various advisories that provide stock, options, and income recommendations—as well as non-market wealth-building advice—to more than 75,000 subscribers.

When founders Mark Ford and Tom Dyson launched Palm Beach Research Group in 2011, they wanted to create a publishing company unlike any other.

Most financial advisories are little more than stock "tip sheets." Mark and Tom had a different vision for their company. They wanted to provide subscribers a comprehensive wealth-building plan; one that would guide readers along the path to real, sustained financial prosperity.

To this end, Mark and Tom focused the Palm Beach Research Group on three key areas... safe income, safe growth, and comprehensive 360-degree wealth building.

Specifically, they've combined Tom's experience in the financial markets with Mark's success as a serial entrepreneur and real estate investor to achieve their goal—a holistic, wealth-building publishing company.

Services now include:

- Stock market investments (long-term and trading)
- Cash-generating options strategies
- Rental real estate investing strategies
- "Outside the market" ideas for generating additional active income
- Credit repair strategies
- Entrepreneurial guidelines on starting your own business
- Retirement lifestyle guidelines.

And much more...

Each service supports the central mission of the Palm Beach Research Group:

Help readers get richer every single year.

To learn more about the Palm Beach Research Group, visit www.palmbeachgroup.com/about.

About the Author

Tom Dyson is the publisher of the Palm Beach Research Group. Tom bought his first stock when he was 11 years old, and he has been studying the art of investing and speculating ever since.

Tom graduated from the University of Nottingham, in the United Kingdom. He's a member of the Chartered Institute of Management Accountants, one of Britain's top accounting bodies. He went on to work for bond trading desks at Salomon Brothers and Citigroup.

For the past six years, Tom has spent his time researching and writing about conservative income investments at Stansberry Research. His income-focused newsletter, *The 12% Letter*, was one of the most popular advisories in America. He still holds several of the "top 10" spots in Stansberry's hall of fame for highest gains on his recommendations.

Today, Tom leads the Palm Beach Research Group, which is not just a stock market investment advisory, but a holistic, 360-degree wealth-building service.

Contents

Introduction

I thought I'd seen it all...

Over the past 10 years, I've examined almost every type of safe income investment in existence.

I've studied utilities, municipal bonds, real estate, and real estate investment trusts. I've researched MLPs, BDCs, and royalty trusts. I've dug into CDs and bank deposits. And I've analyzed almost every well-known dividend-paying stock in America.

And before that, I worked for two of the world's largest banks—Salomon Smith Barney and Citibank—in London.

So I must admit, when I discovered a secret, high-yield account (what we call the 770 Account) used by more than 3,500 banks, I was a little shocked.

For example:

- Bank of America has $18.5 billion tucked away in these accounts
- Citibank has $4.5 billion hidden in its own secret accounts
- And JPMorgan Chase conceals $9.8 billion in this type of account

They'd put more of their money in these accounts if they could, but regulators restrict them from putting more than 25% of their safe core capital (referred to as Tier 1) here.

You see, just like IRAs, Roth IRAs, and 401(k)s, the 770 Account lets you grow your money tax-free.

That's why top bankers and Fortune 500 executives in the know have quietly been taking advantage of opportunities like these for years now...

Safely earning generous yields on their money—up to 5% on average—while everyone else has been stuck chasing low-paying CDs, bonds, and dividends.

Now, tax-free returns of 5% may not sound like much, but if you're in a 35% tax bracket, that's the equivalent of earning close to 8% in your regular taxable brokerage account.

At first, when I first discovered this secret from my colleague Tim several years ago, I was a little skeptical...

But I knew Tim was a smart guy... and I couldn't ignore it.

Tim recommended an obscure book that explained the account and this strategy in more detail.

How obscure?

There are 136,450 books for sale on Amazon with the words "real estate" in the title.

There are 65,137 books on Amazon with the words "stock market" in the title.

But there are fewer than 15 books I know of that discuss this idea...

I looked up the book Tim recommended. Amazon didn't have it in stock, but I was able to buy a 10-year-old used edition for $5.

A few weeks later, I sat down and read it...

I was intrigued, so I didn't stop there. I tracked down a few other books on the subject and read those.

Then I wrote to five or six of my contacts in the finance business to get their opinions on this idea. (This includes Mark Ford, my longtime business partner—who has more knowledge of financial products than anyone else I know.)

None of them had heard of this particular idea.

I couldn't find any articles about this in the newspapers and magazines. And I couldn't find any advertisements for it.

In short, this idea is so underground, the only way you'd ever hear about it is if you stumbled onto it by accident. Even then, you'd be unlikely to get involved unless you invested the time to understand its full power. (There are no glossy brochures with bullet-points to explain how it works.)

So I contacted Tim again. He had been using this account himself. And he shared everything he knew. He also put me in touch with an expert who has helped some of the wealthiest people in America set up and use this account.

Within a few weeks, this expert flew to Delray Beach, Florida, and spent the afternoon in my conference room, explaining the details and answering all of my questions.

Finally, I was convinced. And excited. I made two decisions. To do it myself, for the benefit of my family. And to share it with Palm Beach Research Group readers...

Why was I so convinced? Why was I so excited about what I learned?

I'd found the most versatile financial account I'd ever encountered...

> **Note:** The 770 Account has several nicknames. Palm Beach Research Group readers and my colleagues around the office refer to it by its most common name, "Income for Life." Throughout the rest of this book, I'm going to refer to the 770 Account as Income for Life.

PART 1:

Income for Life Uncovered

CHAPTER 1

The "Swiss Army" Knife of Financial Accounts

Today, I'm going to tell you about the most powerful savings account I've ever come across, the 770 Account (what I call "Income for Life"). But it's more than just a savings account. To demonstrate how versatile this account is, I'm going to use a little analogy...

The Swiss Army knife is arguably the world's most popular pocketknife. You likely own one. The dark red handle. The white cross. The multiple tools and mechanisms.

The knife originated in the 1880s when the Swiss army decided to purchase a new folding pocketknife for its foot soldiers. The original Swiss army knife had a blade, reamer, can opener, and screwdriver.

Soldiers could open their canned food. They could repair their rifles. Or they could use the knife blade for dozens of other tasks.

Today, the Swiss Army knife is a robust and versatile tool. Multipleblades, tweezers, toothpick, saw, magnifying glass, screwdriver, pliers, corkscrew, and ballpoint pen to name a few.

A dozen tools, three dozen applications. All in a compact pocketknife. An all-in-one solution in case you need it for the random task or situation that pops up.

Now, as I studied Income for Life, I compiled a list of its many benefits. Its multiple uses and versatility left me with one conclusion: Income for Life is the financial equivalent of the Swiss Army knife.

With Income for Life you can...

- Grow your money at up to 5% over the long term
- Have a contractual guaranteed minimum growth rate of 4%
- Compound your money tax-deferred (pay no taxes on gains each year)
- Completely avoid risk of principal loss—meaning you can sleep at night knowing your account balance won't go down in value (even if the stock market crashes 50% tomorrow)
- Safeguard your money in a place with a century-long track record of safety.

It's such a safe vehicle that you can also...

- Protect your money from creditors or lawsuits (in most states)
- Contribute unlimited amounts to it (unlike an IRA or 401(k))
- Avoid reporting it to the IRS come tax time
- Access your money anytime without penalty or withholding taxes
- Build a line of credit to use for any reason—no questions asked.

As you can see, there are so many benefits to Income for Life. Two different people might choose to open an account for totally different reasons. That's one of the things that makes it such a powerful financial tool.

I'm not going to get into the details of each benefit here. That will come later. Instead, right now, I'd just like to focus on two of my favorite benefits. One, Income for Life's safety. And two, the way it enables me to maintain 100% control over my money—accessing it whenever I want.

Let's talk about safety first.

How to Instantly Protect Your Money Forever

At the Palm Beach Research Group, we place an enormous emphasis on teaching our readers to avoid risk and keep their money safe.

A big part of that is making sure people know the difference between saving and investing. Most financial planners use the terms synonymously. But that's inaccurate. Saving and investing have distinct differences.

The primary purpose of investing is to *grow* your capital. The primary purpose of saving is to *preserve* it. As any stock market crash will illustrate, preserving your capital doesn't always happen when you're investing.

Over your investing career, understanding this distinction could mean the difference between financial success and failure.

Take my dad. He learned this lesson the hard way.

My father retired on New Year's Eve 1999. As an investment banker on Wall Street during an economic boom, he'd spent the previous 10 years working harder than he'd ever thought possible... and getting paid more than he'd ever imagined.

At the age of 52, with several million dollars in "savings," he decided it was time for a new, more leisurely lifestyle. He hung up his suits, threw out his alarm clock, and began composing poetry and oil paintings.

But his money wasn't in "savings" at all. He'd put all of his money in the stock market... and concentrated it in several bank stocks, including Lehman Brothers.

Think back to when you were a teenager saving for your first car. Did you give the money you were saving to a friend so he could start a new business? No! You put it in a safe place, like a bank account or a sock drawer.

You put it in a place where there was no chance you would lose any of it, where you could add to it when you needed, and where you could access it whenever you wanted it.

Well, my dad didn't do this. Turns out, he had his "savings" invested in the worst possible place—a company that was about to go bankrupt.

In the crash of '08, Lehman Brothers folded, and Dad lost almost everything. Most of his life savings vanished.

He has had to go back to work... as a piano teacher. If he'd put that money into true savings vehicles, where there was no risk of loss, he'd probably still be retired.

As you can see, the distinction between savings and investing is a distinction of purpose. Savings is money earmarked for certain future expenses. Investing is extra money set aside simply to build wealth... after you've taken care of your saving and spending.

These different purposes demand different strategies. Saving requires a very low degree of risk. Investing allows for some—but not too much—risk.

As an investor, you can put your money into a wider range of stocks—including some that you believe will "outperform" the market, such as some of the recommendations we publish at Palm Beach Research Group like in *The Palm Beach Letter* or *Mega Trends Investing*.

Or you can buy real estate that you believe will appreciate in value. Or you could fund a private business that you believe in. Or you can trade options. And so on. (We cover all these strategies.)

But here's the thing... Investments will always be subject to loss. The business you invest in could fail (nine out of 10 startups fail). The stock you invest in could go belly up. The stock market could crash, just like it did in 2008.

Your savings, on the other hand, should be very safe. It should be trusted to only the sturdiest possible financial vehicles. There should be no risk that you'll lose it.

It wasn't just my dad who made this mistake. Tens, even hundreds of thousands of retirees worldwide made the same one.

In fact, I'll bet many of you reading this haven't yet distinguished between saving and investing—you may have ALL your retirement money invested in vehicles such as 401(k)s and IRAs, or ALL your children's education expenses in Coverdell or 529 plans.

Almost all of these vehicles are in stock market-related investments like mutual funds or stocks. But this money should also be in savings vehicles.

This is one of the reasons why I was so drawn to Income for Life—my money is totally safe. That's because this account has no exposure to the stock market. If the Dow crashes 50% tomorrow, my account balance won't drop a single dime.

Many of the companies that administer these accounts have safely grown investors' savings for over a century without default.

With this strategy, there is virtually no risk of principal loss. Like a bank account, your money will never go down in value.

And you'll always have full control over your money.

Unrestricted Access and Control

The second benefit I'd like to briefly touch on involves my ability to access my money.

I'm 38. I've got three young kids and a full life ahead of me. I'm thinking a lot about my financial future. Saving for retirement. A new house. Generally, I don't believe in college, but I'm considering setting aside some money for my kids if they want to go.

If I follow mainstream financial advice, how do I plan for these life events? Well, I should have a 401(k) and maybe an IRA to save for retirement. If I'm considering savings for my kids' college, I'll open a Coverdell or 529 plan. A new house? I'd better save up for a down payment and make sure my credit is up to par for my future mortgage.

But there's always been something very unsettling to me about these options.

What if I wanted to retire when I was 50? I'd have to pay steep penalties to access my 401(k) or IRA funds before age 59.5. What if I didn't want to retire or need to access the money in my retirement accounts? It wouldn't matter; the government would force me to take that money at age 70 so it could collect its taxes.

What if my kids didn't want to go to college? I'd have to pay penalties to access the funds in those 529 accounts.

What if I had an unexpected medical emergency expense? Same thing, I'd have to pay penalties to access my money to handle that.

Though I have some of these accounts, I've never liked the lack of control. I've never liked all the rules and restrictions that come with them. And I've never liked having all my money scattered amongst these separate accounts.

As I dug deeper into the details of Income for Life, I discovered that it offered me complete control of my money. Because of a special set of features, it can act as a central warehouse for my money. Using the strategies I read about, Income for Life gives me the flexibility to use it for any financial life event... virtually anything I could imagine.

It could act as my retirement plan. Meaning I could get the bulk of my retirement income from it in the future.

It could act as a college savings plan for my kids.

I could use it to pay for any big-ticket expense. A vacation. A down payment on a house. A new car.

I could leverage its funds to invest in anything... rental real estate, stocks, options, or precious metals.

I could use the funds to start a business. Or loan money to a friend or family member.

I love this kind of control. I can let my money sit—or I can access it at any point, no questions asked, in less than three days.

This has actually become my single-largest investment...

And we've coined a term for this strategy... "Income for Life."

Today I have more than 75% of my total net worth allocated to the Income for Life strategy... and I'm still adding money to it. I've made it the foundation of my retirement strategy.

I've even opened up Income for Life accounts for each of my three children;

and because of this decision, they'll now be financially set for life. (My oldest son, for example, will have about $4 million in his account by the time he retires.)

Before I tell you what this is all about, I need to explain why your money is so safe in these accounts.

CHAPTER 2

The Safest Place on the Planet for Your Money

We're putting our money into a special type of dividend-paying company. You've probably never heard of these companies, even though they're among the oldest in America. Most financial professionals haven't heard of them, either.

I made a list of 35 of these special companies doing business in America today. The oldest company on the list is 177 years old. The average age of these companies is 106 years. Nineteen of them have been in business for more than a century.

These companies are rare. No one has formed one in a very long time (worldwide), and no new ones are likely to ever be formed again.

These companies do NOT trade on the stock market. Their values don't fluctuate like traded stocks.

They don't use debt.

Acquiring one of these companies is very difficult. This is why Wall Street has no business with these companies. And it's why you've probably never heard of them.

And, of course, they generate tons of cash, and they pay large dividends to their owners every year.

They make up the world's safest industry.

The companies I'm describing are a special breed of life-insurance company. Now, I know what you're thinking...

Most financial gurus say life insurance is a bad place for your money.

But please bear with me.

The companies we discovered are not your run-of-the-mill insurance companies. I'll explain why they're different from regular life insurance companies in a moment. In fact, these companies behave much more like savings or investment accounts than insurance companies. However, the government restricts the advertising these companies can use.

But first, let me explain why life insurance is such a great industry for safety-conscious investors...

Life insurance is one of the oldest financial products in existence. The sale of life insurance in the U.S. began in the late 1760s. It has proven itself through two world wars, a revolution, a civil war, the Great Depression, and numerous recessions.

Even though some insurance companies have gone under (like AIG in the 2008 financial crisis) there have been very few life insurance contract defaults in the last 300 years in America.

Can you think of any other product that has proved itself like this? Popular investment products today include mutual funds, ETFs, 401(k)s, and IRAs. None of these products have been around longer than a few decades.

Life insurance is a recession-proof business. People need it regardless of what's going on in the economy. It's also a mathematical business, like running a casino, but with even better odds. As long as you price your risk correctly and you don't do anything stupid with the premiums you collect, you won't lose money over the long term.

Of all of the different types of insurance companies, life insurance companies are the safest.

Consider common insurable events, such as fires, earthquakes, and hurricanes. They're rare. Which means scientists have fewer examples to study. The damage claims can be astronomical. And you can't predict when these types of events will occur.

Now consider life insurance. A person's death is certain. Life expectancy is predictable for large groups. There's plenty of data. And the insurance company knows what the payout for death claims will be.

Demand for life insurance never changes. It stays constant in a recession or an economic boom. This industry doesn't have a business cycle.

Statistics drive profits in this industry. As long as their equations are accurate—which they are, because they've been using them successfully for decades—they make predictable profits.

Insurance companies hire data-crunching experts called "actuaries." Actuaries study this data. Then they create life insurance policies for the insurance company's customers. As long as the actuaries do their jobs and the insurance company has enough customers, you can virtually guarantee it'll be profitable.

During the Great Depression, more than 9,000 banks went bankrupt. According to a hearing of the Temporary National Economic Committee in 1940, only 2% of the total assets of all life insurance companies in the U.S. became impaired between 1929 and 1938.

Because the life insurance industry was so strong, it played a big part in keeping the country afloat and helping many troubled businesses get back on their feet.

One example is department store mogul James Cash Penney. The great stock market crash of 1929 almost wiped out J.C. Penney. He was able to borrow funds from his life insurance company against his policy to keep his small department store chain in business through the Depression. Today, J. C. Penney has 1,000 stores and is worth $3.4 billion.

The same pattern appeared after the stock market crash of 2008-2009. We examined several of the safest insurance companies and found that less than 1% of their investments were listed as "nonperforming" during the financial crisis.

Not only did the recent financial crisis not affect these insurance companies, but they also continued their century-long track records of paying dividends. If I had to bet on a group of companies being around 100 years from now, I'd choose these.

But, as anyone who invested in MetLife stock knows, not all insurance companies are equal. MetLife's stock crashed 80% between 2008 and 2009.

MetLife is one of the largest and most popular life insurance companies today—but that didn't prevent its investors from losing a lot of money.

For our Income for Life strategy, we're interested in only a tiny—much safer—subset of the life insurance industry.

These companies aren't as well known as MetLife—but they are very safe, and they pay out a lot of their earnings, as well.

There are two types of life insurance companies: stock life insurance companies and mutual life insurance companies.

Stock life insurance companies trade on the stock market. They issue stock, and they trade like any other public company. Hartford, MetLife, and Prudential are all stock life insurance companies.

Mutual life insurance companies do not trade on the stock market. They don't have shares, and you can't buy into them through the stock market. They're like credit unions, except the policyholder is an owner in the insurance company.

Mutual life insurance companies are much safer than their "stock-issuing" cousins.

For one thing, because mutual companies have no shareholders, Wall Street analysts and money managers cannot pressure management to make short-term decisions. The companies are free to pursue long-term strategies. As a result, these corporations are known to be among the most conservatively managed companies in the world.

Stock life insurance companies have millions of shareholders. Many of these shareholders are powerful money managers. They want higher returns on their investments. It encourages the management of stock life insurance companies to take risks.

Mutual life insurance companies serve only one master... the policyholder. There are no outside shareholders to split profits with. No Wall Street. No quarterly earnings estimates. No conference calls. No insider trading. No takeovers. No message board gossip. No stock options.

Think of mutual life insurance companies as cooperatives... or not-for-profit clubs. A bunch of people have come together and pooled their money to provide life insurance for themselves.

Safety, stability, and good service are the only goals of the insurance company. Mutual insurance companies still generate profits. But these get distributed back to all of the members each year as dividends. We'll get to dividends in a minute.

You're more likely to see stock insurance companies borrowing money, advertising, and using

STOP: READ THIS—Your Top Objections Answered

I know you may be shocked to hear Income for Life involves a type of life insurance.

But don't let this put you off. The Income for Life strategy is not about life insurance at all—it's about the foundation it's built on. We use this special type of insurance like a car frame. You can build an average car or a sports car on the same frame.

We take the same life insurance framework and use it to build a financial vehicle with qualities we want. We design it in a special way to compound our money at up to 5% per year, tax-free. This unique type of life insurance account is the best vehicle we know of to guarantee growth and provide safety.

We've spent huge amounts of time, energy, and money researching this topic.

We've disproved many of the common myths and overcome many objections you are sure to have.

Read the rest of our research. And when done, if you're still skeptical, you can read through our top questions and answers at the end of the book.

other aggressive growth strategies. They'll invest in riskier assets to appease hedge funds or large shareholders with higher returns.

They're also more likely to fudge their quarterly earnings releases to make their results seem better.

In sum, mutual insurance companies are one of the safest places on the planet to put your money. And one of the highest-paying places, as well.

Keep reading... I'm going to explain how you can use mutuals as "secret savings accounts" that offer the guaranteed growth of our money for the REST OF OUR LIVES.

These accounts can pay up to 5% tax-free per year.

It All Started as a Bet on One Man's Life

Before we continue, we'll get a quick history lesson on life insurance.

The life insurance business started as a wager.

On June 18, 1583, a London man named Richard Martin placed a bet with a group of merchants. The bet was on the life of another man, named William Gybbon. Martin put up 30 pounds.

If Gybbon died within one year, Richard Martin would make 400 pounds. But if Gybbon did not die, Martin would lose his 30-pound stake.

Gybbon died just before the end of the year. But the merchants refused to pay Martin his winnings. So Martin took them to court. The court ruled in favor of Martin. And the merchants' payment became the first official life insurance payout.

The modern name for this type of life insurance agreement is a "term" policy.

Putting the above example into contemporary terms, Richard Martin was the "policyholder" and "beneficiary" of the policy. The 30 pounds he paid was his "premium payment." The merchants were the insurance company.

And we'd call William Gybbon the "insured."

Term insurance is just a simple bet. It's the policyholder betting against the insurance company. The policyholder is betting on a death, usually his own. And the insurance company is betting on survival.

If the insured person dies in the allotted time or "term," the policyholder wins the bet (and the beneficiary gets the money). If the insured survives, the insurance company wins the bet and the policyholder loses his stream of payments.

Please note, buying term life insurance is a bet the policyholder expects to lose, but it's still a bet. But he's willing to take this bet because it's cheap. And he can provide his family with financial protection if he dies.

Today, term policies are the most popular type of insurance policy, representing just fewer than 40% of all life insurance premiums paid in America each year. (Today it's most common to buy 10- or 20-year term policies.)

But here's a fact that may shock you.

Only 3% of the term insurance contracts conclude with a payout. What that means is the insurance company "wins" the bet 97% of the time!

Early in the 19th century, insurance companies invented a new type of insurance policy. They called it permanent insurance.

Permanent insurance is an insurance contract that remains in force until the insured dies. It has no term. It's permanent.

Because there is a 100% chance that the insured will die, permanent life insurance is NOT a gamble; it's a certainty. You buy $1 million of permanent life insurance. As long as you don't cancel the policy and you make your premium payments, the insurance company is going to pay out $1 million someday.

To pay out $1 million when you die, the insurance company must accumulate at least $1 million while you're living in order to make the payout and not go out of business.

It accumulates this money by collecting premiums from you each year. These premiums build up over time, and they generate interest—which also builds up and compounds. By the time of your death, you've built up plenty of money at the insurance company so it can pay your policy off.

To reinforce this point:

In order for the insurance company to pay out your life insurance policy when you die, it must first accumulate this money while you're alive. It does this by collecting premiums from you each year and investing them.

When you boil permanent life insurance down to its basic cash flows, first you make a series of payments to the insurance company while you're alive. The insurance company collects these payments, grows them, and then gives them back to you at the end of your life.

In other words, permanent life insurance has almost nothing to do with life insurance. It's a way while you're alive to save money that your heirs get back when you die.

Do you see that?

Permanent life insurance is a certain payment to you from the insurance company in the future. This money exists because you've saved it up—and the insurance company has grown it—over many years.

In this way, permanent life insurance has nothing to do with life insurance. It's about saving money. It's a glorified bank savings account with a much higher interest rate.

In contrast, term life insurance is a wager with the insurance company whether or not you'll die in a given period. Term life insurance is not a vehicle for saving money. It's a way to protect your family in case you die unexpectedly.

As you can see, a permanent life insurance contract is really a strategy for saving up money over time so that the insurance company can pay out the full amount when you die.

Here's the beautiful part...

While you're accumulating money with the insurance company, your money earns interest.

Due to special tax provisions for insurance companies, this return is tax-free.

When you buy your policy through a mutual life insurance company, you become an owner of the company. As an owner, you receive a share of the profits your company generates via a dividend.

In fact, we studied eight companies that provide these policies, and they have now paid out, on average, for 121 years in a row.

When I add it up right now, the money I have in Income for Life is generating a return of 5% per year, tax-free, after dividends and interest.

But I know you have one major objection to this plan. If you're like me, you're probably thinking:

"Why would I put my money into an investment that pays only when I die?"

This is a great question. And the answer is very simple. The way permanent life insurance works is that you can use the money you're accumulating at the life insurance company anytime you want. You can do this through something the experts call a "policy loan."

Not one in 100 people know this, but you can use your Income for Life policies to pay for just about anything...

People use these policy loans to pay for vacations, cars, houses, and medical expenses. You can also use these loans to finance any future investments in stocks, real estate, or small businesses.

By running these expenses through your Income for Life policy, you can generate an enormous positive cash flow. And eventually, no one in your family will ever have to borrow money from a bank or financing firm again.

I won't get into the details of this strategy yet. For now, all you need to know is that you can use the money you've saved anytime you want. You can do this with no penalty and no fees, as if it were sitting in a bank account.

And even while you're using it, it keeps growing up to 5% per year.

But not all life insurance is created equal. Most of it is too complex to understand. So let's talk about the type that you should be looking for.

CHAPTER 3

A Century-Long Track Record of Dividends

Three years ago, my wife and I met with a life insurance salesman in Jacksonville, Fla. He was trying to sell us a permanent life insurance policy.

We spent two hours in his office. He spent the first hour asking us dozens of personal questions about our finances. This made us uncomfortable.

He spent the second hour pitching us on a life insurance product involving the stock market. It was so complex that he used a thick binder and several glossy brochures to explain it to us.

Both of us left the meeting annoyed and confused. We decided we would never buy permanent life insurance. "We'll never understand it," we said.

I'm certain complexity is the biggest reason people hate permanent life insurance.

Insurance companies have sold permanent life insurance for centuries. But over the last three decades, they've made "innovations" to the original model. This has hurt its reputation.

For example, today, insurance companies sell policies in which you can adjust how much money you get when you die. Or when you pay the premiums. You can buy policies that pay interest based on the stock market's performance... or the bond market's performance.

You may have heard of some of these innovations. They have names like universal life, variable life, equity indexed universal life, etc.

In short, these innovations have introduced hundreds of variables into permanent life insurance policies. The customer can't understand them. Most agents don't understand them. And most importantly, they have shifted the risk away from the insurance company and back to the policyholder.

Plus, the complexity makes it easy for the insurance company to hide the fees and commissions it's charging.

This was a big reason my wife and I wouldn't buy life insurance. I couldn't understand the fees the company wanted to charge me.

I'm not saying you couldn't structure an Income for Life strategy with a universal, variable, or equity indexed life insurance policy. But I'd advise you not to. They're too complicated.

Here at the Palm Beach Research Group, we hate complexity. One of the rules Mark and I established when we first launched the Palm Beach Research Group was we'd never recommend anything we couldn't understand and explain in simple terms.

At its core, our Income for Life strategy uses the most ordinary type of permanent life insurance. It's the Coca-Cola Classic of the insurance industry. Its design hasn't changed in over 100 years.

Read on to understand how it works:

First, you agree with the insurance company how much money you want to receive when you die.

Then you pay a minimum amount every year into your policy. They call these payments "premiums." You agree to these amounts up front with the insurance company. They never change.

While you're alive, these payments build up a cash value in your policy. And you earn interest and dividends, tax-free, on this cash. Meanwhile, you can also use this money whenever you need it.

That's it.

There are no fancy customizations. And it has nothing to do with the stock market. But it's easy to understand. It's been tried and tested over two centuries. And, set up the way we recommend, it comes with some of the lowest commissions of any permanent life insurance product on the market.

In the industry, they call it "whole-life insurance." Whole-life insurance is a common insurance product. You can buy it from almost any insurance agent in the country... or around the world.

Our Income for Life strategy uses a "participating" or "dividend-paying" whole-life insurance policy. And you become a part owner to share in the profits.

When you own a participating whole-life insurance policy, you become a part owner of the insurance company. That means you're entitled to a share of the profits. Profits come from two places, underwriting and investments.

Now, most insurance companies have several lines of business. They'll issue term policies. Or they'll offer employee benefit programs that offer medical, dental, and disability insurance.

They might issue auto policies. And most have retirement divisions that offer things such as 401(k)s, annuities, or long-term care solutions.

If insurance companies underwrite and manage these programs the right way, they'll pour money into their own coffers. And the only customers of the life insurance companies who share in the underwriting profits—the ones these multiple lines of businesses generate—are the ones with "participating" whole-life policies.

The second way insurance companies generate profits is from their investing activities. Think of the hundreds of thousands of customers an insurance company has. All of these customers make annual, quarterly, or monthly payments to the insurance company for all of the policies they have.

That means there's a steady stream of cash pouring into the company each day. The insurance company won't need to pay many of its claims immediately. It takes years, sometimes decades, for people to collect.

Instead of sitting on this cash, insurance companies conservatively invest and grow it. They know with exact precision when they'll need the money to pay claims.

At the end of each year, the insurance company tallies the profits from its investing and underwriting activities. It pays expenses and claims, then sets aside a little into a reserve account for extra safety. What happens to the rest of the profits?

They're dispersed to "participating" policyholders as a dividend each year.

The top mutual insurance companies we recommend are so prudent at managing their investments and insurance businesses that they've managed to pay dividends to participating policyholders for more than 100 years in a row.

> **Note:** When a mutual insurance company issues a whole-life policy, it calls it "participating" or "dividend-paying" whole-life insurance. It's called "participating" because policyholders own the mutual company and participate in the profits by earning interest and dividends.

There's one final twist we'll add to the basic structure of a dividend-paying whole-life insurance policy. This twist makes it different from any other type of life insurance policy, including most of the whole-life policies the industry sells today.

CHAPTER 4

How to Use the IRS's MEC Ruling to Your Advantage

Call up your local life insurance agent. Ask him for a whole-life insurance policy. He'll sell you the life insurance coverage that comes with a savings component.

But we've established that Income for Life is NOT primarily about the life insurance coverage.

What do I mean by this?

Most people think of life insurance as something you buy to protect your family in case you die. It's a precaution. But our Income for Life strategy has very little to do with estate planning, protection, or life insurance.

It's a program to save money and build wealth *while you're still living.* We structure our whole-life policy to emphasize the savings aspect and minimize the life insurance aspect.

In the insurance industry, they'd say we're trying to "maximize the cash value of the policy and minimize the life insurance coverage."

We do this by stuffing as much money into our whole-life policy as we can, as quickly as possible, keeping our life insurance coverage as low as possible.

For example, a typical term life insurance buyer might pay $1,000 per year for a $2 million policy.

But we would prefer to pay $20,000 per year for a $500,000 whole-life policy. This way, we get much more money earning interest and dividends, and we give much less money to the insurance company for life coverage.

Do you see this?

Most people want as MUCH life insurance coverage as possible by spending as LITTLE money as possible.

With our Income for Life strategy, we want to get as LITTLE life insurance coverage as possible, by putting as MUCH money as possible into our policy.

Income for Life uses a special tool to make this happen. It's called a paid-up additions (PUA) rider. Most mutual life insurance companies offer this rider. But few insurance agents know it exists. And if they do, they don't know how to maximize its value.

A PUA rider is a way to stuff as much money into your policy as is legally possible. This way, you're earning more interest and more dividends in your account, without increasing the amount you spend on life insurance protection.

I'm not going to get into all of the details of the PUA rider just yet.

For now, all you need to know is that the PUA rider changes an ordinary whole-life insurance policy into a wealth-building machine.

What do I mean by, "stuffing as much money in your policy as is legally possible"?

Insurance policies confer enormous tax benefits. In the '70s and '80s, investors and corporations plowed billions into permanent life insurance policies to take advantage of the tax benefits. In 1986, the IRS clamped down. It set a limit on how much cash you could put into permanent life insurance.

If you exceed this limit, your life insurance policy turns into what the IRS calls a "modified endowment contract," or "MEC" for short. And it won't qualify for the tax benefits.

The illustration below shows the relationships of insurance types to this MEC line. At the bottom of the chart, you have term insurance. It offers only insurance, and it's the cheapest. There is no savings component with term insurance.

Wealth Building or Life Insurance Coverage?

Income for Life uses as little life insurance coverage as possible, without breaching the IRS's MEC rule

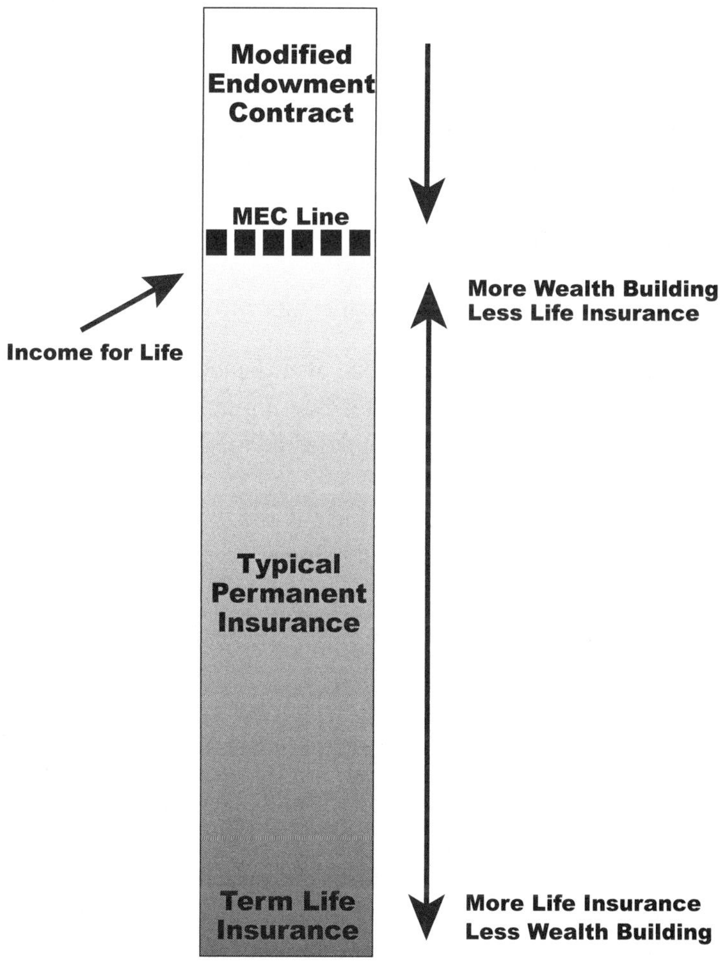

At the top of the scale, you have insurance policies that offer 100% savings with the least amount of life insurance. These are MECs.

In between, you have various other types of permanent life insurance.

The thick dotted line shows where an insurance policy turns into an MEC and loses its tax benefits (tax-free growth).

Income for Life uses a participating/dividend-paying whole-life insurance policy from a mutual insurance company. We use a PUA rider to put as much money into our whole-life policy as we can WITHOUT crossing the MEC line.

The fact that the government limits how much money can be put into this insurance policy should show you how powerful this strategy is.

In summary, Income for Life is a unique savings strategy that uses one of the oldest, most tried-and-true products in existence... whole-life insurance. We set it up using a very specific tool that not one in 99 insurance agents knows about (using the PUA rider).

Again, with this special type of account you can:

- Grow your money at up to 5% over the long term
- Have a contractual guaranteed minimum growth rate of 4%
- Compound your money tax-deferred (pay no taxes on gains each year)
- Completely avoid risk of principal loss—meaning you can sleep at night knowing your account balance won't go down in value (even if the stock market crashes 50% tomorrow)
- Safeguard your money in a place with a century-long track record of safety.

Your money is also fully accessible, and safe, as you can also:

- Protect your money from creditors or lawsuits (in most states)
- Contribute unlimited amounts to it (unlike an IRA or 401(k))
- Avoid reporting it to the IRS come tax time
- Access your money anytime without penalty or withholding taxes
- Build a line of credit to use for any reason—no questions asked.

Ready to get started? Let's talk about what you need to know in order to open your own policy.

PART 2:

Income for Life Explained

CHAPTER 5

The 5-Minute Primer

> *Tom, the one thing I want Palm Beach Research Group readers to know is that Income for Life is a lifelong commitment. They shouldn't be putting money into this if they don't have the discipline to stick with it.*

Mark Ford is my business partner here at the Palm Beach Research Group.

Mark is no industry novice. He's a self-made multimillionaire who has successfully started several of his own businesses and invested in dozens of others over the last 30 years. He's also an experienced real estate investor. If there's one thing about Mark I've learned, it's that he hates to lose money. Because of that, he's very skeptical about any investment or financial strategy he's not familiar with. Income for Life was no exception.

Yet after I taught Mark about Income for Life and conveyed to him all the benefits attached, Mark is now ready to officially endorse it to Palm Beach Research Group readers.

But Mark has made it clear we need to explain all the details of these insurance policies. It's critical that people know exactly how these policies work, over what time frames, and what the eventual results will be.

Why?

You see, insurance products can be very complicated. Opening a policy is not like buying a stock or mutual fund. It's much more involved. And to complicate the matter further, insurance companies don't disclose much information to consumers about how their products work. Plus, agents can easily manipulate or take advantage of uneducated consumers.

> **Note:** The Income for Life experts we recommend to our readers don't fall into this category, of course. They set up policies the way we recommend... the way gives consumers the highest amounts of cash. They use the simplest and easiest-to-understand type of insurance. And our experts will always be available to answer your questions about minimizing fees.

Now, Mark's point about sticking with your policy for the rest of your life is very important. In fact, it's so important, it bears repeating: The only acceptable holding period for your insurance policy is <u>forever</u>. If you do not plan to hold it for that long, don't do it.

There are a handful of other important concepts you need to understand before you even pick up the phone to have your first conversation with an Income for Life expert.

So let's start with the first concept—you're going to hold your policy forever.

You're excited about putting money into Income for Life. You've allocated $10,000 for your new policy. You're ready to write a check and sit back to watch your money grow.

Not so fast...

With a stock, you can click a button in your brokerage account and buy $10,000 worth of a company. Purchasing a bond might take a little more work, but in general, it's a simple process. If you want $10,000 of gold, you can walk into your local coin dealer and buy it.

But with Income for Life, it's different. You can't click a button, make one payment, and be done.

The Income for Life strategy involves putting your money into a dividend-paying whole-life insurance policy from a mutual insurance company.

A whole-life insurance policy is a contract between you and the insurance company.

When you open a policy, you agree to pay your insurance company money each year (or month). In return, the company promises to grow that money each year until the contract matures. Typically, that's between ages 100-121.

If you die before you reach the insurance contract maturity date/age, the insurance company agrees to pay you (or whoever is the beneficiary of the policy) the contractual death benefit.

The point is this: Your Income for Life policy is a contract that lasts for life. And because of how the insurance company structures the contract, it requires you (the policy owner) to make a payment each year.

Now, it's not as bad as it sounds. While a whole-life insurance contract does last for life, that doesn't necessarily mean you'll be writing checks from your bank account each year to pay the insurance company.

There's all kinds of unique and flexible ways to fund and pay for a whole-life insurance contract. (We'll get into these details in an upcoming section.)

But Mark's point remains—if you can't commit to keeping your contract forever, don't put money into an Income for Life policy. It's important that you go into this with the right mindset: Once you open your policy, you're going to want to keep it open for life.

> **Key Takeaway:** If you don't have the discipline to stick with your policy for life, you shouldn't put money into Income for Life. If you terminate your policy before, say, 10 years, you will lose money.

Now, how will you know how to set up and fund your Income for Life contract? You and your Income for Life expert will need to come up with a unique plan to allocate money into your whole-life insurance contract.

How much you allocate will depend on your personal financial position. You and the Income for Life expert will discuss questions like, how much money do you have saved right now? How much money can you save each month going forward? When do you plan to retire? When will you need income?

Now, in order for you to get the most out of this conversation, it's going to help if you're familiar with some terminology that's specific to insurance contracts.

Having a thorough understanding of these terms and ideas will enable you to be certain you're setting up the policy in just the right way for your personal financial situation.

To help you understand these terms, we've compiled a terminology primer.

A whole-life insurance contract comes with an "illustration." An illustration is a spreadsheet of numbers that projects how your policy might perform over the coming years.

In short, it's the insurance company saying, "Based on where interest and dividend rates are today, if you give us this set of annual payments, your account will be worth the following amount at the end of each year."

The insurance company then proceeds to list your account balance in the policy at the end of each year (after you make your annual payment).

The illustration has three main columns you need to know about.

Premium

The first is the "Premium" column. This is the money that the insurance company requires you to pay each year.

Think of this just like your monthly auto insurance premium. Or your annual home insurance bill. Or your monthly health insurance premium.

You and your Income for Life expert will decide ahead of time how much your premium will be.

Cash Value

The second important column is "Cash Value." This is the money available in your account. Think of it like your brokerage or bank account balance. It will grow each year. Right now, most mutual insurance companies will grow the cash in your account at long-term rates up to 5% per year when you factor in guaranteed interest and dividends.

Keep in mind, your personal returns will depend on your age, sex, and health rating.

Death Benefit

The third important column is "Death Benefit." This is the money your family or designated beneficiary will receive if you die before your policy matures (remember, your policy's maturity age will likely be between 100-121 years).

We don't put money into Income for Life with the primary purpose of getting insurance or death benefit protection. But it's a great side benefit. And if you're older or retired, your policy can be a useful tool for retirement planning.

So, we have three important columns. To recap...

Premium is the payment you make each year.

Cash Value is the balance or money in your account in any given year.

Death Benefit is the money your spouse, family, or beneficiary will receive if you die before your contract matures.

> **Key Takeaway:** An illustration is not a guarantee of exactly how much cash value your policy will have each year. It's a snapshot of what could happen if interest and dividend rates stay the same every year during the life of your policy.

Your cash value could end up being lower in the future (if interest and dividend rates go down). Or your cash value could be higher (if interest and dividend rates go up).

Now that you have a better understanding of the key terms in your policy, let's discuss a point you and your Income for Life expert will need to address: the different types of insurance premium payments. If you structure your payments the wrong way, or leave some of them out, you'll end up with a poor and inefficient policy.

CHAPTER 6

Insider Secrets—Slashing Fees up to 70%

Income for Life is a way to grow your money—while safeguarding it from any risk of loss. But one of the most compelling features of Income for Life is being able to access the money built up in your account whenever you need it.

Here's the thing: If you rely on just any regular insurance agent to set up your policy, you'll have to wait years, even a decades, to build up a decent amount of cash value for your personal use.

But when you set up your policy the Income for Life way, you'll have gobs more cash to use right away.

It all comes down to how your agent structures the premium payments of your policy.

You see, regular agents often set these policies by applying 100% of the premium payment to what insurance companies call "base premium."

Allocating all of your premium payment to base premium will get you the maximum amount of insurance or death benefit possible. If that's all you're after (and there are some cases this might make sense), great.

But base premium does two negative things. And they're interrelated.

First, maximizing your base premium means you'll pay the highest amount of commission possible to the insurance agent. Because of that, the cash buildup in your policy during the beginning years is horrible... almost nonexistent.

Look at the example below. It gives you the numbers on a policy for someone close to my age (35) and health rating (to be covered later) with a $10,000 annual premium. I set it up to apply 100% of my money to "base premium."

Mainstream Policy Setup

100% of Total Premium Goes to "Base Premium"

Age	Year	Annual Premium	Cash Value	Death Benefit
35	1	$10,000	$0	$998,991

Notice the cash value column. After making a $10,000 premium payment, I've got $0 of cash value. Now, the benefit of this is that I have an immediate death benefit of almost $1 million.

In other words, this type of payment structure is great if I open a policy for the death benefit. But it's terrible if I want to be able to access my cash value.

There's one small change an agent can make to the premium payment structure. It'll slash his commission up to 70% and give you immediate cash value in your policy. Making this small change will totally transform a policy into something that doesn't resemble regular whole-life insurance.

What is this small change? It's the addition of a rider into the annual premium schedule. It's called the paid-up additions (PUA) rider.

The regular way to set up whole-life insurance is to allocate the full $10,000 to base premium. Remember, that buys as much death benefit as possible.

Instead, an agent can elect to allocate a large percentage of your total premium payment to this PUA rider.

Look at the example below. It's the same policy from above, but I structured the premium payment so that I apply only $3,000 of the total

$10,000 amount to the base premium. I apply the remaining $7,000 to the PUA rider.

Income for Life Policy Setup

70% of the Total Premium Payment Goes to the PUA Rider

Age	Year	Annual Premium	Cash Value	Death Benefit
35	1	$10,000	$6,832	$324,450

Notice the cash value column this time? There's immediately $6,832 available for use the day after I make my $10,000 premium payment.

Now, do you also notice the death benefit? It's $324,450. There's much less death benefit. Why? It's because we applied only $3,000 of the premium payment to the "base premium."

But that's fine, because—remember—the death benefit isn't the primary reason we opened this policy in the first place.

What I want you to see is how one simple modification in the structure of the premium payment and the PUA rider instantly transforms your policy.

Why not apply all of the $10,000 of your premium payment to the paid-up additions rider?

Well, you could, but then you'd lose the tax benefits. The IRS would tax you on the growth and dividends in your policy every year. To keep the favorable tax benefits where your money grows tax free, the IRS requires that you keep a certain amount of insurance. We'll cover this topic in the next section.

As an analogy, think of the total premium payment as a dial or slider on your stereo system. Turning the dial all the way to the left would maximize the bass of your stereo; turning the dial all the way to the right would maximize the treble.

Of course, as you know, too much bass leaves your music muddled and distorted. Too much treble leaves the music tinny and hollow. Usually, moving the dial to somewhere in the middle gives you the best sound.

Think of your total premium payment the same way.

If you turn the dial all the way to the right (allocate 100% of the premium payment to "base premium") you'll have $0 cash in your policy the first year.

It will take much longer to build any meaningful cash value in the early years. The graphic below shows this.

All Base Premium

Allocating 100% to "Base Premium" Gives You $0 Cash, but Lots of Insurance

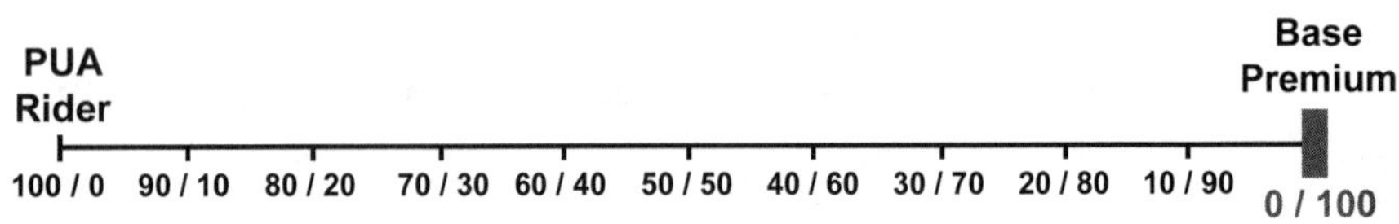

Now, turn the dial to the other end, all the way to the left (allocate 100% of the premium payment to the paid-up additions rider).

This time, you'll have close to or 100% of what your first year premium payment was. The graphic below shows this.

All PUA Rider

Allocating 100% to "PUA Rider" Gives You Almost All Your Cash to Use Right Away

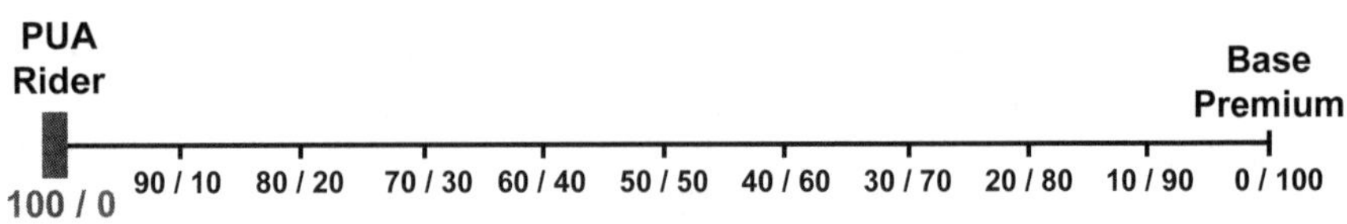

But your insurance policy will then be a modified endowment contract, or MEC. That means you won't get the tax-free growth benefits. And then anytime you want to use your cash value, you'll have to pay income taxes on your gains each year.

The goal in most cases is to dial your setting a bit to the left to include as much PUA rider as possible without losing the tax benefits.

In our example Income for Life policy above, I was able to make the premium payment a 70/30 split. Meaning I allocated 70% of the total premium payment to the paid-up additions rider. Then 30% to the base premium. Any more than this and I would have violated the modified endowment contract limit and lost the tax benefits.

How much should your Income for Life expert apply to the PUA rider when designing your policy?

It'll depend on your age, sex, health rating, and overall financial strategy. A good rule of thumb is to have 50-70% of your total premium payment go to the PUA rider, as illustrated in the graphic below.

The Right Mix of PUA Rider & Base Premium

Allocating 50-70% of Your Total Premium Will Give You the Most Amount of Immediate Cash Without Losing the Tax Benefits

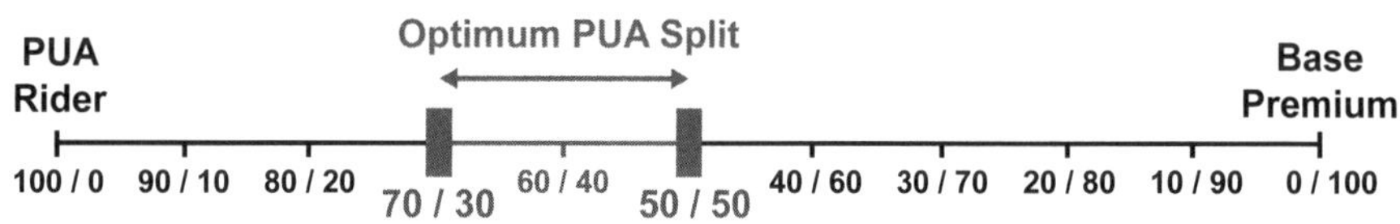

Now, to understand how your agent should set up your policy's premium payments, you need to understand the MEC limit. We'll cover that next.

Key Takeaway (No. 1): The more of the total premium payment dedicated to "base premium," the higher the agent commission and the less cash value you'll have in the early years.

Key Takeaway (No. 2): The more of the total premium payment dedicated to "PUA rider," the lower the agent commission and the more cash value you'll have in the early years.

CHAPTER 7

Revealed: Income for Life's Only Disadvantage

I have one significant frustration with Income for Life: Once I set up my policy, it isn't easy to put more money into it.

What do I mean by that? If I came into some money (maybe a work bonus, gift, or inheritance) I could transfer it to my brokerage account. Then I could immediately place a trade and buy more stock.

But it's not that easy with a whole-life insurance policy. If I just sent the insurance company extra money to deposit into my account, I could trigger a disastrous result—a permanent loss of my tax-free growth benefits.

This has to do with the MEC limit that I referenced in the previous section. The IRS implemented this MEC rule for life insurance contracts in 1988. Why?

Prior to this, the wealthy stuffed billions of dollars into life insurance because of the favorable tax benefits. The IRS started to ask questions:

"Wait, these people are setting up insurance contracts with massive paid-up additions. They're stuffing tons of cash in there so they never have to pay taxes on it. And there's hardly any death benefit.

"These contracts don't look anything like a life insurance policy. We're going to put a stop to this. And going forward, we'll require a minimum level of life insurance in these contracts."

I'm paraphrasing, of course. But that's what happened. The IRS required that certain levels of death benefit exist in a policy to keep the tax-free growth benefits.

If you had too little death benefit, your policy would be considered a modified endowment contract. And you'd lose the tax benefits. But if you stayed below this MEC limit, you'd keep your tax benefits.

I'm not going to get into all the complexities of this rule. All you need is a general understanding of this MEC limit and how it affects your insurance contract. Then note it and make sure you never pay premiums of more than this amount in any given year.

How do you know what this annual dollar limit is?

Every insurance contract comes with an illustration. Remember, that's the summary of your premium payments, cash value, and death benefit.

Every illustration will also list this MEC limit. Look for the "7-pay premium test" section on your illustration. That's IRS jargon for the MEC limit. It's the dollar amount the IRS will allow you pay into your policy each year without violating your MEC limit.

If you're working with one of our Income for Life experts, they'll make sure to set up your policy so it's not a MEC.

Now remember, the premium payment dial graphic I showed you earlier? This MEC limit is what affects how much your expert can allocate to the PUA rider.

Here's the Income for Life policy setup using a PUA rider...

Income for Life Policy Setup

Allocating 70% of the Total Premium Payment to the PUA Rider Is the Most I Can Do Without Going Over the MEC Limit

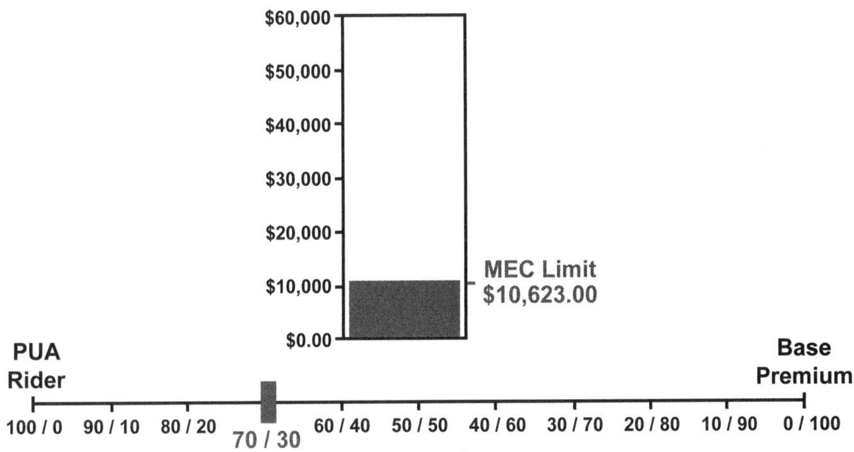

Remember how I said I applied 70% of my $10,000 premium payment to the PUA rider?

Well, I couldn't allocate any more than that to the PUA rider. That's because my MEC limit was $10,623. Any higher allocation to the PUA rider would have resulted in the IRS viewing my insurance policy as a modified endowment contract. And that would mean I'd lose my tax-free growth benefits.

But this poses a problem... and it's one my frustrations with Income for Life. What if, say, in year two of my policy, I received a $5,000 gift from my grandparents? Or maybe I received a bonus from work?

The only way for me to put it into Income for Life would be to open another policy. That means another application, medical exam, and long underwriting process. That's quite a nuisance compared to the ease of putting that money into my brokerage account.

But there is a way to increase the MEC limit. What I'm about to tell you will provide some room to add money to my existing policy in the future. And I won't go over the MEC limit.

It's good to know in case you want this flexibility.

So how do you set up a policy to allow more room for future payments?

Here's our premium payment graphic again. The way to increase the MEC limit is to turn down the dial on your PUA payment just a little bit. In other words, you would allocate a little less to the PUA rider and a little more the base premium.

Here's an example...

Income for Life Policy Setup

The More Base Premium You Include, the Higher Your MEC Limit

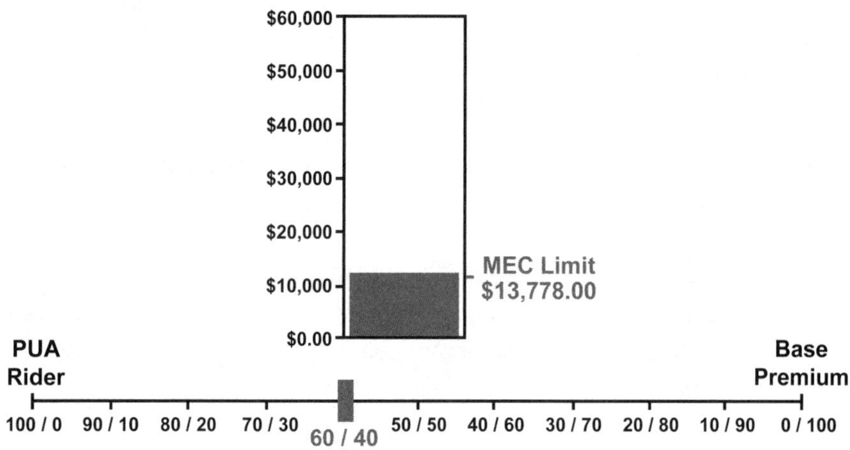

By changing the split to 60/40 (60% of my premium payment to the PUA and 40% to base premium), I increase my MEC limit to $13,778.

Though my annual premium is $10,000 a year, I can add an additional $3,778 each year and NOT go over the MEC limit and lose my tax benefits.

Here's another example, this time using a 50/50 split.

Income for Life Policy Setup

The More Base Premium You Include, the Higher Your MEC Limit

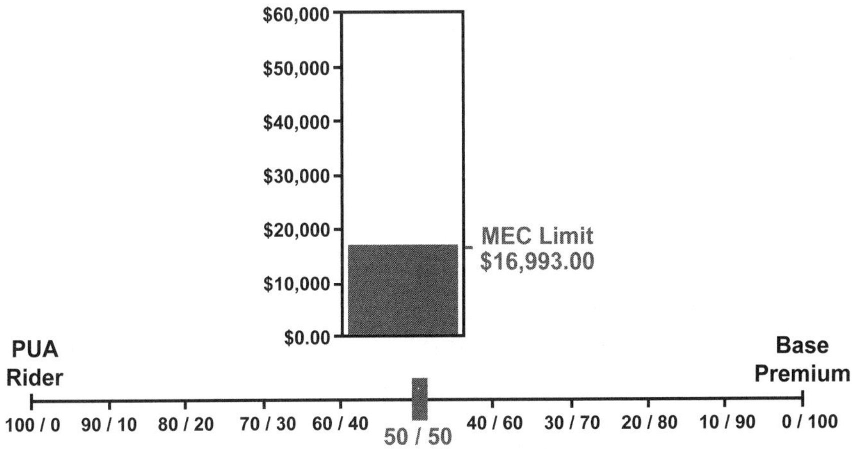

By changing the split to 50/50 (50% of my premium payment to the PUA and 50% to base premium), I increase my MEC limit to $16,993.

Though my annual premium is $10,000 a year, I can add an additional $6,993 each year and NOT go over the MEC limit and lose my tax benefits.

Are you starting to see how the total premium payment slider dial works with the MEC limit rules?

Now, while it's nice to have the ability to put unexpected money in an existing policy (instead of having to start a new policy), there is one downside.

Remember that if you allocate more of your total premium payment to base premium (sliding the dial to the right) the agent commission is higher. And as a result, you'll have less cash value to use right away.

As I mentioned, a 50/50 split (50% PUA rider and 50% base premium) would give me only $4,880 of cash value in the first year. In this scenario, the MEC limit is the highest of our three examples ($16,993).

If I bump it up to a 60/40 split (60% PUA rider and 40% base premium) I'd have more cash value in my first year—$5,856. In this case, our MEC limit drops to $13,778.

And finally, with a maximum amount of PUA rider (70/30 split), I'd have $6,832 of cash value in the first year. Here, the MEC comes in at the lowest of the three values at $10,623.

So, as you can see, there's a tradeoff. The higher MEC limit that allows me to put more money in my policy gives me less cash value up front with my regular annual payments.

Key Takeaway (No. 1): Make sure to pay attention to the MEC limit of your policy—and be certain you never pay in more than this limit in any given year.

Key Takeaway (No. 2): If you want as much cash as possible as soon as possible, make sure your agent allocates as much to the PUA rider as he can without going over the MEC limit. But know that you won't have any room to add additional money to your policy above your regular annual premium payment.

Key Takeaway (No. 3): If you don't need maximum cash value as soon as possible and you want some room to add money to your policy in the future, make sure your agent allocates a little less to the PUA rider.

Now that you understand how premium payments work in relation to the MEC limit, it's time to talk about common objections to whole-life insurance.

PART 3:

Income for Life Decoded…
Your Top Questions Answered

CHAPTER 8

The Biggest Lie in Modern Finance?

I want to bust one of the biggest lies in modern finance.

That is: Putting money into dividend-paying whole-life insurance (the type we use with Income for Life) is a big mistake because of its high fees and commissions.

In an earlier chapter, I told you that some years ago, my wife and I were shopping for life insurance. (This was before I knew about the Income for Life strategy.) A friend had referred us to an agent at a well-known insurance company.

He was trying to sell us a whole-life insurance policy. My wife and I were getting frustrated with how much he pried into our finances. And he was taking up too much of our time.

I knew the perfect question to end the meeting...

"So how much commission do you make from this policy?" I asked.

"I take a 100% commission," he replied.

I was expecting a high number, but this seemed impossible.

"100%?"

"That's right," he said. "We take 100% of your first year's premium payment as a commission."

"No wonder everyone thinks permanent life insurance is a rip-off," I thought. And with that, we excused ourselves and left.

Life insurance companies have a reputation for charging the highest commissions in finance.

This reputation is so bad, there are pages and pages on Google with titles such as "Why You Should Never Buy Whole-life Insurance" and "10 Reasons Permanent Life Insurance is a Scam."

There are even two popular finance gurus—Dave Ramsey and Suze Orman—who actively campaign against permanent life insurance because they say the fees are so high.

It's Not Really 100% in the First Year

Talk to any life insurance agent and there's a 99.9% chance they'll set up a policy with the same fee structure as the agent I just mentioned.

The Income for Life experts we recommend at the Palm Beach Research Group all use a special rider when they design policies. It's called a PUA rider. Set up the right way, this rider lowers the first year's fee substantially and turbo charges the cash buildup in the initial stages of the policy. That's why it's critical that you use one of our recommended experts.

And earlier, a popular newsletter writer published an article criticizing whole-life insurance (which is what we use in our Income for Life strategy). He didn't like the fees—among other things.

As with most things in finance, to get the truth, you have to crunch the numbers.

So that's what we did.

I asked my colleague Tim Mittelstaedt to show me the actual fees I'd paid on a whole-life policy I recently opened with a well-known mutual insurance company our experts recommend.

Tim is our director of new product development at Palm Beach Research Group. When I hired Tim in 2011, I tasked him with understanding everything he could about insurance. I wanted him to have access to all the data directly from the insurance companies that regular consumers like you and I could never access. And so he became a fully licensed life insurance agent.

Tim went to my mutual insurance company's website and downloaded the details of the fees I paid. As it turns out, the fees I'm paying for my policy are among the lowest fees I've ever seen on any investment or savings product—including ETFs and no-load mutual funds—in the entire investment universe.

Here's what Tim came back with...

> Tom, you're putting money into your dividend-paying whole-life policy as follows:
>
> For Years 1-4, you structured your account with four annual lump-sum deposits of $50,000 per year. And then, starting at Year 5 and moving onward, you'll deposit $17,500 per year. Your contributions look like this:
>
> Year 1-4: $50,000 annually
>
> Year 5-50: $17,500 annually
>
> Over those 50 years, you'll pay a total of $1,005,000 into your policy. And through the magic of compounding, it'll be worth $5,707,219 (but that's a story for another day)...
>
> You're paying fees (commissions) as follows:
>
> Year 1: $17,494
>
> Year 2-10: $875 per year
>
> Year 11-50: $175 per year
>
> Over 50 years, you will pay a total of $34,319 in fees to the insurance agency that set up your policy.

Then I asked Tim to calculate the fees I would have paid if I'd put the same amount of money into a low-cost bond fund or ETF that makes the same return...

At their core, they do the same thing. A mutual *fund* company has a manager who allocates investors' money with the intent to grow it over time. A mutual *insurance* company invests, manages, and allocates the money customers pay in premiums with the intent to grow it over time.

And besides, the fee mechanism mutual funds use is very common throughout the financial industry. It's Income for Life's biggest competition, in other words.

Here's what Tim came back with:

> According to Morningstar, the average expense fee (called the annual expense ratio) for bond mutual funds is 1%.
>
> To contrast that, the average expense ratio of the mutual funds offered by our company's 401(k) plan through Fidelity is over 2% per year. Many other mutual funds have similar costs.
>
> And let's assume the bond fund generates the same long-term return as your whole-life insurance policy. (I used 5.2%. That's the annual growth your policy projects each year over this 50-year period... after fees.)
>
> I used the exact same deposit amounts, as follows:
>
> Year 1-4: $50,000 annually
>
> Year 5-50: $17,500 annually
>
> The total cumulative amount you'd pay into the bond mutual fund over 50 years would be the same: $1,005,000.
>
> Through the magic of compounding, your account would be worth $5,707,219—exactly the same as the Income for Life strategy.

> You'd pay a fee every year. And the fee would get bigger every year as your account grows...
>
> In Year 1, you'd pay $526.
>
> In Year 2, you'd pay $1,074.
>
> In Year 3, you'd pay $1,645.
>
> In the first 10 years, you'd pay total cumulative fees of $25,189.
>
> In the first 20 years, you'd pay total cumulative fees of $88,326.
>
> In the first 30 years, you'd pay total cumulative fees of $205,742.
>
> In the first 40 years, you'd pay total cumulative fees of $404,930.
>
> How much would you have paid in total fees over 50 years in the bond mutual fund?
>
> $727,311.
>
> That's over 20 times the $34,319 you'll end up paying in life insurance fees over the same period.
>
> More importantly... that 1% mutual fund fee caused a difference of more than $1.8 million in final account value. The mutual fund investor has an account with $3.9 million. The Income for Life policyholder has an account value of $5.7 million.

This was astonishing, even to us. But there's no mistake. Let me explain why that little mutual fund fee does such big damage.

There are two ways you can extract fees from an investment...

First, there's the standard mutual fund way, which is now the standard Wall Street way. Once per year, they assess your fee based on the total amount of money under management. It could be 1% per year. Or 2% per year.

The great thing about this method for Wall Street is the fees get bigger and bigger as your money grows. They compound. This is Wall Street's little secret.

The money you inject into the account is assessed with fees over and over again, every year.

I never realized how devastating these "little" annual fees could be until I started investigating this issue. They look small and insignificant, but they're not.

Look at this chart. The black dots represent your account growth over time in a mutual fund-based fee structure. And the gray dots represent the fees your account generates. Look how the fees grow in size as your account value grows in size.

How Fees Accumulate in a Traditional Investment Account (401(k), mutual fund, etc.)

In a traditional investment account, the account manager takes a percentage of the account balance in fees. As the account balance grows, the account manager's fee grows.

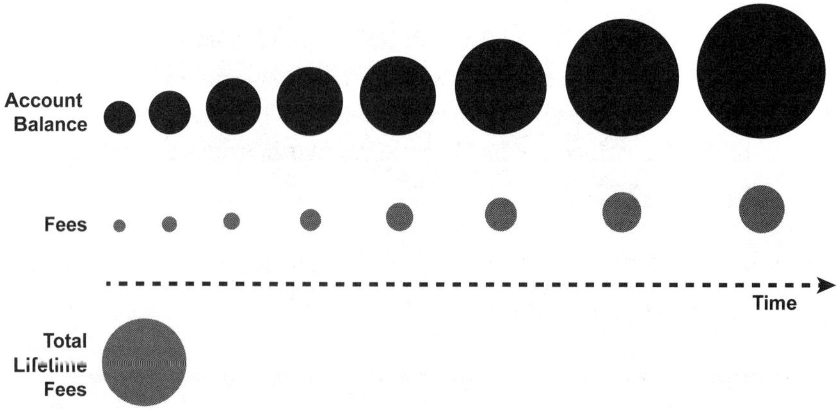

Then there's the life insurance method of charging fees. First, the insurance company bases its fees on the money you put into the policy each year, not the account's total value.

Then the insurance company front-loads the fees. So I'm paying a 33% fee up front on my first payment, then a 5% fee for the next nine years. And then a maintenance fee of 1% for the remainder of the policy. To clarify again, that's only on the money I put in... the annual premium payment, not the entire account size.

How Fees Accumulate in a Whole-life Insurance Policy

In an Income for Life policy, the fee the life insurance company charges you has nothing to do with your account balance. It's based on the money you pay in, using a fee schedule that tapers off.

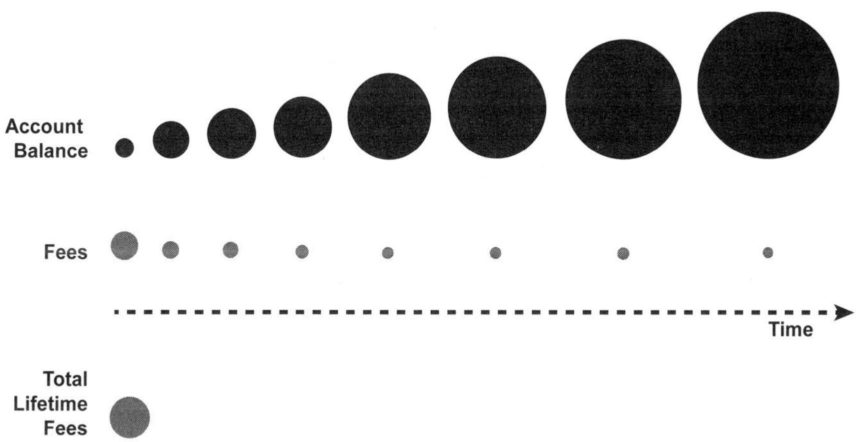

This way, over time, the fees shrink instead of grow. Look how the fees get smaller with each passing year with the life insurance method of charging fees.

It's a vital distinction. And it makes an enormous difference. How big?

Look at both charts again. At the bottom of each chart, there's a gray dot that represents the total lifetime fee each method generates. After 50 years of collecting fees, the mutual fund's gray dot is 20 times larger than Income for Life's gray dot.

Or, consider the numbers from our simulation. Investing the same dollars at the same time and growing them at the same rate, the mutual fund generates $662,992 more in fees. And because the fees hinder the compounding, we end up with $1.8 million less in the account after 50 years.

I can't claim all life insurance products have low fees. Some products and policies have higher fees than others. And there are agents who don't care about their customers and sell them unsuitable policies to generate higher fees.

All I know is that dividend-paying whole-life insurance with a paid-up additions (PUA) rider—the strategy we use in Income for Life—is the oldest, most basic type of permanent life insurance in existence. And I'm happy to pay the fees. I'm getting a great product and great service in return. You should be, as well.

I wish those gurus who trash whole-life insurance were more concerned with the fees people pay on their mutual funds and in their 401(k). Because whenever you pay a fee based on your total account value—even if it seems like a small percentage—you're getting ripped off.

That's because the fee compounds as your money does, and it eventually becomes enormous.

But why do life insurance companies charge fees, anyway?

Like any business, they need to cover their costs. They pay salaries. They own buildings. They buy advertising. They offer sales incentives.

But life insurance is a great, efficient business. It doesn't require expensive financing from banks, because it has its own river of cash—as policyholders pay premiums every year.

It doesn't operate any heavy industry. It's never building plants or making other long-term investments that take years to pay back.

There's no retail presence, so life insurance companies don't have to maintain giant branch networks to attract customers.

It's a mature industry. Many of the players have been in business for more than 100 years. They know how to keep costs down by operating their businesses efficiently.

It's a competitive industry, which makes it efficient and transparent.

And the business never changes because it's based on the one certainty in life: death. So there's no technical obsolescence to worry about. And insurance companies never need to invest in research and development.

So it doesn't make sense that life insurance companies would charge higher fees than other asset management companies in particular, and other financial companies in general. If anything, they charge lower fees because they're more efficient.

But consider this:

First, the government regulates life insurance fees and commissions. An agent would lose his or her license—and maybe even go to jail—if regulators caught him or her overcharging customers. Or undercutting the competition by reducing fees or offering kickbacks.

It's illegal for a life insurance company or agent to charge anything but the state-regulated fee.

Second, my life insurance agent is providing a great and valuable service to me. Not only did he spend time and money to set up my policy, he will take care of my family and me for the rest of our lives—providing advice and helping me administer all my policies.

Relative to the small fee I'm paying, I'm getting a great deal.

Third, there are many types and variations of life insurance. Most were invented in the 1980s and 1990s during the craze for financial engineering. We don't recommend any of these complicated, higher-risk life insurance strategies.

The type we use—dividend-paying whole-life insurance from a mutual insurance company—is the oldest, simplest, most vanilla-type of life insurance in existence.

The structure we use has been around for more than three centuries. And when it comes to fees, whole-life insurance (with the special PUA rider our experts use) is the absolute cheapest, most efficient policy you can buy. It has no bells or whistles.

But finally, and most importantly, when you set up a policy the Income for Life way, through a mutual life insurance company, you become an owner in the company. That's because the policyholders own the company. It's the insurance version of a credit union.

The insurance company exists for the benefit of the policyholders. Period. It's like a non-profit. And at the end of the year, management takes all excess capital generated by the business and distributes it back to policyholders in the form of dividends.

So there's no point in the company overcharging the policyholders for their policies, because the policyholders own the company anyway.

The bottom line is this: When you think it through from a business perspective, it makes no sense that life insurance—when set up the Income for Life way—would be a rip-off.

I'm not defending the entire life insurance industry. Far from it.

Every year, life insurance companies come up with ways to "engineer" new, more complicated life insurance products. Universal life insurance is one example of this. Its performance is linked to the performance of the stock market.

And there are many others.

Life insurance agents can make more commissions by selling these products. So that's what they pitch to their clients. And as soon as they've gotten the client's signature, they disappear. This behavior gives the industry a bad reputation.

So long as you stick to dividend-paying whole-life insurance—the most basic type of life insurance—and use one of our recommended experts to set up your policy, you have nothing to worry about.

That's exactly what America's largest buyer of life insurance knows—and profits from.

CHAPTER 9

Where the Banks REALLY Keep Their Money

Who are the biggest consumers of permanent life insurance (the type of insurance we use with our Income for Life strategy)?

When you see how much permanent life insurance these people buy—and why they buy it—you'll never see permanent life insurance as death protection again.

You'd never guess it... but the biggest consumer of permanent life insurance is banks.

Look at this list.

Bank	Life Insurance (Billions)	Bank Premises & Other Fixed Assets (Billions)
Wells Fargo	$19.3	$8.1
JPMorgan Chase	$9.8	$10.2
PNC Financial	$5.9	$4.1
Bank of America	$18.5	$10.9
Citibank	$4.5	$4.3

Source: Barry James Dyke, *The Pirates of Manhatttan II*, 2012

It shows five of the largest banks in the U.S. The first column shows their investments in permanent life insurance. The second column shows their investments in properties, premises, and other fixed assets.

According to FDIC records, the largest 38 banks in America have invested a total of over $100 billion in permanent life insurance.

Sixty-eight percent of these banks have invested more money in permanent life insurance than they've invested in skyscrapers, IT networks, or bank branches.

Your local community bank buys permanent life insurance, as well.

Here are five much smaller banks and the amounts they've invested in permanent insurance relative to their fixed assets.

Bank	Life Insurance (Millions)	Bank Premises & Other Fixed Assets (Millions)
First Republic Bank	$43.2	$10.3
People's United	$29.3	$32.3
City National Beverly	$13.8	$12.6
First Tennessee Bank	$56.7	$33.0
New York Community	$68.5	$22.0

Source: Barry James Dyke, *The Pirates of Manhatttan II*, 2012

Why do banks buy so much life insurance?

It's simple. Regulators require banks to keep large piles of cash on hand to meet unexpected obligations. They could take sudden losses on loans. Or more depositors than normal could ask to withdraw their money.

Think of it as a cushion. This cash cushion must be unassailable. Banks must be able to access this cash immediately. And they cannot put it at risk.

Regulators call this money "tier one capital." And by law, a bank must always keep at least 4% of its assets as tier one capital.

Would money invested in stocks count as tier one capital? No. Stocks are too risky and do not meet FDIC liquidity tests.

What about real estate? No. It takes too long to sell real estate in an emergency.

What about permanent life insurance? Yes! Regulators consider permanent life insurance safe and liquid enough to count as tier one capital.

Permanent life insurance has an additional benefit over cash. It pays much more interest... and there is no tax on either the income or the final payouts.

With these qualities, it's no wonder banks pour money into life insurance. It's so attractive, the Federal Reserve had to make a rule to limit how much life insurance banks buy.

As of 2004, banks can keep a maximum of only 25% of their tier one capital in life insurance.

But wait...

Banks aren't the only companies that spend billions on permanent life insurance. Many non-financial corporations buy it as well. These companies include Comcast, GE, Gannett, Johnson & Johnson, Harley-Davidson, Verizon, Norfolk Southern, and Wal-Mart.

Wal-Mart used to buy permanent life insurance on every Wal-Mart employee *in secret*. When some families found out about it, it caused a scandal. It seemed Wal-Mart was profiting from the deaths of its employees.

But the government clamped down on this practice in 2006. Now companies can buy life insurance only on their top-third highest income earners... and the employees have to agree to it.

Why do Wal-Mart and these other companies buy so much permanent life insurance?

These companies aren't banks. They don't hold tier one capital. But the reason is the same. Permanent life insurance is the highest-paying and safest place for their capital. They can access it anytime they want. And it's tax efficient.

But there's another important reason that banks and corporations spend billions on permanent life insurance. It's the perfect way for them to cover their executive pension obligations.

Aaron Kushner, chief executive of Freedom Communications, says this in a recent article:

> *Companies and banks say earnings from the insurance policies are used to cover long-term health care, deferred compensation, and pension obligations.*
>
> *Life insurance is one of the ways of strengthening the long-term health of the pension plan and ensuring its ability to pay benefits.*

What does this mean? It means these banks and corporations primarily invest in permanent insurance for one reason: to fund pension plans for their top executives.

When a senior executive at a large corporation retires, the company pays him or her a pension. Pension benefit packages include things like a continuing salary, a parting bonus, and health benefits for life.

These pension obligations can be huge. Some executives have pensions that are almost as large as their paychecks were. The former CEO of GE, Jack Welsh, retired over a decade ago. He reportedly earns $9 million per year in pension from GE.

Pensions for average-income earners in America have all but disappeared. But pension benefits for high-level executives are increasing.

Corporate treasurers have found that permanent life insurance is the perfect tool to fund these pension obligations.

Companies can deposit money into life insurance contracts annually. Then they can let the money grow tax-free... much like an IRA. Then the pension administrators can use the cash in the insurance policy to pay the pension while the executive is living.

And when the executive dies, the company receives a large, tax-free lump sum. It can put this toward other employee benefits.

This is interesting because permanent insurance is not what Wall Street and the mainstream financial media advise you to do when you're saving for retirement. Instead, they advise you to turn to stock market-related vehicles like mutual funds, 401(k)s, and stocks.

Don't you find it interesting that when it comes to saving for their top executives' retirement, banks and corporations stay away from the stock market?

Instead, they store that money in permanent insurance... where there are guaranteed returns and no risks of loss.

In sum, permanent life insurance is ultra-safe. And it's easy to access in emergencies. It grows tax-free, and then comes back tax-free upon death. And it offers much higher returns than cash.

Corporate America takes advantage of these benefits. Why shouldn't we?

As I said, there are many objections given by popular media sources. But they're all mistaken. Let me explain why...

CHAPTER 10

Five Reasons the Top Critics Are Wrong

The critics are at it again...

Recently, I came across a 2013 article from a popular money manager repeating the same false idea often found in mainstream media:

> *Whole-life insurance is a more complicated product than term life insurance. Like universal life or variable life universal insurance, whole-life offers an insurance payout and, over time, the policies accrue a cash value that can be withdrawn.*
>
> *The cash value helps financial advisors and insurance agents position whole-life insurance as a type of investment product.* **We believe *whole-life does not make sense as an investment product.***

With a simple Internet search, you'll find dozens—even hundreds—of similar articles, studies, and blog posts that attack whole-life insurance.

One argument is that fees are too high. The "financial gurus" tell you that you are better off buying cheaper term insurance and investing the difference.

What does "buying term and investing the difference" even mean?

The critique from the article above goes like this...

A healthy 30-year-old male will pay $672 annually for a 20-year term life insurance policy. However, the same male would pay $8,230 annually for a whole-life insurance policy.

That means whole-life insurance is $7,558 "more expensive" each year.

The skeptics argue you should buy the cheaper $672-per-year term insurance... then invest the extra $7,558 each year in the market (stocks, mutual funds, ETFs, or some combination).

They claim that over the long term, you'll fare much better. For example, the study referenced claims you'll have $77,000 more after 20 years of "buying term and investing the difference."

This is probably the most common objection we receive to our Income for Life strategy.

Today, I'm going to address the objection that you should buy term insurance and invest the difference. I'll give you five reasons it's invalid...

No. 1: It's Not About the Life Insurance

First, every single "buy term, invest the difference" case study I've seen assumes one thing: Your purpose in buying life insurance is to have a death benefit. You want a lump sum of money for your family in case you suddenly pass away.

And there's nothing wrong with that. Having some life insurance to help deal with a sudden loss in your family is smart planning. Term insurance is the cheapest way to get that protection.

But the amount of death benefit insurance has little to do with our Income for Life strategy. We're not putting our money in dividend-paying whole-life insurance for this death benefit protection.

Why are we paying money into whole-life insurance, then? Because it's one of the safest places to save money. And a dividend-paying whole-life insurance policy comes with nearly a dozen great benefits you can't find anywhere else.

Remember, with Income for Life, you can:

- Grow your money at up to 5% over the long term
- Have a contractual guaranteed minimum growth rate of 4%
- Compound your money tax-deferred (pay no taxes on gains each year)
- Completely avoid risk of principal loss—meaning you can sleep at night knowing your account balance won't go down in value (even if the stock market crashes 50% tomorrow)
- Safeguard your money in a place with a century-long track record of safety
- Protect your money from creditors or lawsuits (in most states)
- Contribute unlimited amounts to it (unlike an IRA or 401(k))
- Avoid reporting it to the IRS come tax time
- Access your money anytime without penalty or withholding taxes
- Build a line of credit to use for any reason—no questions asked.

Show me another savings account that offers all these benefits. It doesn't exist. And you keep all these benefits until you pass away. With term insurance, you get none of these benefits.

Notice what you don't see on that list: life insurance. That's because with our Income for Life strategy, you rarely use a dividend-paying whole-life insurance policy as an actual insurance vehicle.

That's why critics comparing term insurance and whole-life insurance are just plain silly. These policies are structured in very different ways. And they're used for unrelated purposes.

No. 2: Whole-Life Insurance IS Buying Term and Investing the Difference

The irony is a whole-life policy is actually one of the best ways to "buy term insurance and invest the difference." That's because the mutual insurance company uses a portion of your premium payment to buy your "death benefit," or insurance protection. Then they credit the rest of your payments to your account.

The investment managers then grow this money in very safe, conservative investments. High-quality corporate bonds. Mortgages backed by valuable real estate. And sometimes a small amount in very high-quality dividend stocks.

It's a conservative strategy with an investment horizon that extends decades into the future.

No. 3: No One "Invests the Difference"

But let's take a moment to consider the counterargument...

Let's say you do believe in the "buy term and invest the difference" methodology. Are you disciplined enough to invest the difference? Do you have the stomach to take every remaining dollar ($7,558) and invest it?

I'm going to argue that no one does this.

Think about it: If you have term insurance, did you get a whole-life insurance quote for an equal amount? Did you calculate the difference in cost between term and whole-life and then invest that money every year? No.

It's a hypothetical example critics love to use. But it's one that I'd wager no one actually follows through on.

No. 4: Stock Market Returns are Similar to Whole-Life Returns

Now, what if you are the exception? What if you did make this calculation AND you invested the difference?

The study argues investing the difference in a recommended fund would grow to $313,939 over 20 years. That translates to an annual growth rate of 7.1%. And you'd have $77,000 more in your account than with a whole-life insurance policy.

Now, the firm that published this study doesn't include any taxes in its projections. But taxes are a real cost when you invest in a taxable account. You must account for them if you're going to compare a taxable investment account to whole-life. That's because money in a whole-life insurance policy grows tax-free. This creates an illogical apples-and-oranges comparison.

We've researched the true returns of whole-life insurance over the long term and proved you'd need to earn 7.5% in an alternate taxable account to equal the returns of a whole-life insurance policy.

[In our study we used a 46-year-old male and covered a 30-year period. If you're older, the returns could be a little lower than the example used.]

When you compare the after-tax returns of money invested in the market and a whole-life insurance policy, they are very similar. An unfortunate—yet crucial—detail this case study forgot to include.

So on a return-versus-return basis, a whole-life policy and the hypothetical investment in a mutual fund are largely equal. That's where the case study stops.

But this is a huge injustice.

That's because it doesn't report all the additional benefits that come with a whole-life policy above and beyond its return percentage. I'm talking about a whole-life policy's loan features.

No. 5: Term Life Misses Tons of Benefits

Let's cover one of the most exciting benefits that come with whole-life insurance...

With the "buy term and invest the difference" strategy, you commit your money to the stock market. If you ever need that money, you have to sell your stocks, mutual funds, or ETFs. When you do that, you interrupt the compounding process.

But when you put money into a dividend-paying whole-life insurance policy, you can borrow money from the insurance company (up to your account value), <u>but the value of your policy will keep growing</u>. There won't be any interruption in the compounding process.

Of course, let's not forget the convenience that comes with this easy access to funds from your whole-life provider. You can borrow for any reason—no questions asked. You'll have your money in a few days. And you sidestep all the red tape of a traditional bank loan.

You could use loans to finance your car purchases. To finance college costs. To invest in blue chip stocks. Or to invest in rental real estate.

And I'll say it again—all the while, your money in the policy keeps growing. You simply can't do that with a stock market-based investment.

Once you understand the unique benefits of a whole-life policy, you'll see why "buy term and invest the difference" just isn't a logical comparison.

There are some other common objections that keep investors from taking advantage of Income for Life. Let's talk about these...

CHAPTER 11

Three Common Objections Squashed

Recently, I received an email from one of our readers, Dan J., that had several objections to our Income for Life strategy. Here is a quick summary of what he said:

> *I understand that there are tax benefits to saving money in Income for Life, but at the end of the day, you are saving money in a company that is turning around and investing in long-term bonds.*
>
> *I believe that long-term bonds are a terrible place for your money today. You argue that in the recent past, Income for Life policies have shown tax-free growth rates of 5% or higher per annum. You don't go into any detail about how. Where's the proof?*
>
> *Those returns happened because we have a 30-year bull market in bonds. During that time, rates have gone from the high teens to the very low single digits. Going forward, Income for Life policies are not going to be able to compound at the great rates of return that we have seen in recent history.*
>
> *Negative returns in the long bond market will crush all of your rosy assumptions about the compounding benefits of Income for Life policies.*

I told Dan I disagreed with all of his points.

Objection No. 1: Long-term bonds are a bad place for your money.

Dan thinks long-term bonds are a bad place for your money. But mutual insurance companies don't invest only in long-term bonds.

We have access to a report that details the investment activities of 100 of the top insurance companies. We looked at the top seven mutual insurance companies' investment portfolios.

They invest only 65-80% of their portfolios in bonds. And in their bond portfolios, they spread money into bonds with varying maturity dates.

In fact, this report shows that the top 100 insurance companies had an average of only 20% of their bond portfolios in long-term bonds (bonds with over 20-year maturity dates).

No one knows what's going to happen with bonds. Sure, there's plenty of evidence that we have a bond bubble and that it will burst. But when? Many well-respected experts called for a bond crash in 2007. Here we are, years later, and that bubble still hasn't popped.

So we're not concerned about the current so-called bond bubble. We know that our money is in the hands of the most conservative and prudent investment managers on the planet.

Many of the mutual companies we recommend have figured out how to navigate bond bear markets, stock market crashes, the Great Depression, world wars, and any other economic or financial crises the world has thrown at them over the last 100-plus years.

How do we know this? These mutual companies have been able to pay dividends to policyholders for more than 100 years in a row.

Look, these mutual companies aren't run by idiots. They're well aware of the bond bubble, as well. And guess what? They're planning and taking steps to prepare.

The top 100 insurance companies have, on average, moved 36% of their bond portfolios into bonds with durations shorter than five years. Some of the mutuals we recommend have as much as 48% of their bond portfolios in short-term bonds.

That means when bonds crash, the companies will be able to roll this money into cheap bonds with much higher yields. And policyholders will reap higher dividends because of it.

It doesn't matter if bonds crash, because insurance companies don't trade in and out of bonds. They are just interested in safe, steady cash flow. So when an insurance company buys bonds, it holds them until they mature.

With their stellar track records and conservative management teams, we're confident our money is safe and will continue to grow. And we love that we don't have to worry about what the markets are doing... or trying to predict what will happen.

Objection No. 2: Our projections are rosy.

Others say that, going forward, whole-life insurance policies won't be able to grow at the rates they have the past 30 years.

If you started a policy in 1981, interest rates were 18%. That means our policy illustration projections reflected these higher rates of return.

Fast-forward to today. You would find that your policy would have not grown as fast as projected because interest rates have gone down since that high in 1981.

But now what you have is the exact opposite situation. Interest rates are at rock-bottom historic lows. And bond yields are low, as well. There's just not much further downside.

We'd argue that now is the best time in recent history to be starting an Income for Life policy, because there's a much higher chance that interest rates will increase in the future. As a result, insurance companies will be able to put their money into higher-yielding investments.

That means the illustrations you're seeing on your policy now could be too low. In 10-20 years, you'll find that your money has grown a lot faster than current projected rates.

Objection No. 3: Our 5% return claim is too high.

Our 5% return projection is backed by a piece of hard evidence. Not a projection or an illustration, but an actual policy that we recently came across that has been active since 1959.

We looked at the last three statements (for 2010, 2011, and 2012) of the policy.

The owner made a $388.40 annual payment every year since 1959. His policy's cash value balance at the end of 2012 was $93,498.

That means it's grown at an annual compound rate of 4.8% per year for 53 years. It didn't quite hit 5%. Why? The owner admitted to taking dividends in cash for some of this time. That means he didn't reinvest them in the policy.

Also, the agent who set up this policy didn't design and set it up the Income for Life way.

Of course, this is looking backward, and there are no guarantees of this level of growth going forward. But a policy that's weathered 50 years of ups and downs is good enough evidence for me.

And remember, you don't lock up your money in a policy. The point is that you can put up the money in your policy as collateral to take out a loan from the insurance company and do whatever you want with it.

We use the analogy that dividend-paying whole-life insurance is like a Swiss Army knife. A multi-purpose tool you can use for dozens of things throughout life.

You might use it to invest in rental real estate for a few years. Then you might use it to finance your kids' college educations. Then, during retirement, you can start taking withdrawals and dividends for income.

PART 4:

An Interview With the World's Toughest Skeptic

I introduced you to Mark Ford, my business partner at the Palm Beach Research Group, in an earlier chapter. He's a notorious skeptic of most kinds of investing and trading strategies. When Tim Mittelstaedt (our resident in-house Income for Life expert) and I first approached Mark about Income for Life, he had several objections.

Below, I've included an interview between Tim and Mark. Mark put Income for Life "on trial" so he could make a decision on whether he'd endorse it or not. If you're still skeptical or unsure about Income for Life, I'm sure you'll find this interview a useful recap.

CHAPTER 12

Income for Life: Does It Make Sense for You?

Way back in July 2011, when we were just beginning the Palm Beach Research Group with Tom, I (Mark) said this about life insurance in one of my *Creating Wealth* essays:

> *You should consider life insurance an expense, not an investment. It is a cost you pay to safeguard against an unlikely event. It is not a good investment, nor is it a good estate-planning or retirement tool. Every nickel you put towards it will probably make you poorer. Use it to insure your life and nothing more.*

So when, in 2012, Tim and Tom told me they wanted to recommend Income for Life to our readers, I objected.

> *"The only sort life insurance we should recommend is term insurance," I told them. "We should tell them to buy term life insurance until they have hit their retirement number and then get out of the life insurance game altogether."*

But they insisted. "If you need life insurance to help a surviving spouse, you're right. Term insurance is the cheapest way to do that," Tim said. "But this is different. This is a savings strategy that provides the tax benefits of life insurance but without the traditionally high commissions. Plus, there's a neat loan feature that comes with the policy. We want to teach people how to use it."

Although I was 100% sure that they believed everything they said, I was not sure that they hadn't missed some of the little tricks insurance companies typically use to hornswoggle their customers.

So for nearly two years, I've been asking Tim hundreds of questions about it—some of them over and over again.

To give you an idea of how this two-year conversation went, here, in condensed form, are the questions I asked and the answers I got...

There Are Guarantees, and Then There Are Guarantees

Me: "Let's start with this guaranteed return. I simply don't believe it. I've bought whole-life insurance before and I've been shown the charts—supposedly very conservative estimates—but the results never equaled the projections."

Tim: "You're talking about the illustration... the spreadsheet that shows what your policy grows to based on what you pay in.

"Well, you're right—the results in that initial illustration will never be identical. You see, those illustrations take a snapshot of what the growth rates are today. What the illustration shows is a projection of what that money would grow to IF growth rates stay where they are.

"Of course, that doesn't happen. Interest rates go up and down. Recessions happen. Stock market booms happen. Some years, an insurance company will have more claims. Some years, less.

"Now, chances are you were pitched a more risky type of insurance product riddled with higher fees, as well.

"We've got access to the results of how quite a few policies have performed. One of the mutual insurance companies we follow performed a study of how projected policy returns measured up over a 30-plus year period.

"For example, the insurance company projected a $250,000 whole-life insurance policy issued in 1980 on a 35-year-old non-smoker. It showed the cash value balance would be $332,426. Based on the premiums this person would pay, that would be equivalent to earning 4.44% on that cash every year for 34 years.

"How did the policy actually perform?

"Well this same policy's actual cash value balance was $433,187. That's the equivalent of a 5.65% return every year for 34 years. That means it's performed better than originally projected in 1980."

(By the way, Tim just told me that he recently discovered his mom had a whole-life policy that she started in 1981. The other day, he crunched the numbers to see what her returns were. Based on what she paid in over the last 34 years, she's earned 5.3% per year on that cash.)

Me: "Okay. So the return on investment is backed by the company itself. How safe is that?"

Tim: "The company has paid policyholders returns every single year since 1860... over 150 years.

"Now, I've told you about the 4% guaranteed returns... but I haven't even mentioned the dividend. When you factor that in, the total growth rate can be 5% or more."

Me: "So where does the dividend come from?"

Tim: "Mutual insurance companies are businesses. They generate income through premium payments coming in from health insurance, auto insurance, home insurance, life insurance. They also earn profits from investing in (normally) safe vehicles such as bonds and other debt instruments.

"On the expense side, they pay out claims when they arise, as well as the normal operating expenses such as salaries, office expenses, and agent commissions.

"They also set aside some of the profit in reserves.

"The left-over profits get distributed to the whole-life insurance policyholders in the form of a dividend.

"Different from the 4% promise, these dividends are not guaranteed. But the mutual companies I have studied have been paying dividends 100-150 years in a row *without a single exception*."

Me: "That's hard to believe. How is it possible?"

Tim: "Keep in mind that these mutual companies aren't publicly traded. They don't have to worry about 'quarterly earnings reports.' The result is more conservative underwriting and investing.

"For example, mutual companies won't issue new insurance policies to just anyone with a heartbeat (as many stock insurance companies do). Instead, they'll spend time and money putting applicants through proper medical tests to properly evaluate risks.

"On the investing side... they won't chase high returns or yields. They'll stick with the safest bonds and debt instruments they can find.

"In other words, these mutual companies take a long-term, multigenerational approach to growing, investing, and keeping policyholder money safe."

Me: "I can see how such a long and unbroken history of payouts to policyholders could give an investor comfort. But times change, and companies change with them. These mutual companies may have been strong for 100-plus years—but how do I know I can count on them in the future?"

Tim: "These are the safest institutions on the planet. They invest in the safest bonds, with a very small portion in mortgages backed by quality A-plus real estate.

"They have been profitable through two world wars, the Great Depression, interest rate shock in the 1980s, and countless other financial disasters. And the most recent financial fiasco—the meltdown of 2008—was no exception.

"I have access to a database that shows how the investment portfolios of these mutual companies performed during that time. One of my favorite mutual companies saw the subprime mortgage crisis coming. Their investment managers pulled all money out of Freddie and Fannie mortgage-backed securities... long before they went bankrupt.

"Not even 0.1% of their invested assets were in default or 'not performing.' That was during the worst crisis since the Great Depression."

Me: "I believe you—but I don't understand how that could be."

Tim: "Don't forget. These insurance companies have lots of reserves. Plus, they aren't allowed to practice fractional reserve banking like banks are... and do."

> Banks are required to keep only 10% of deposits on-hand—or less, depending on the dollar amount of net transaction accounts the institution holds. Some have a "no minimum" reserve requirement. But the maximum reserve requirement is 10%. Basically, this means that at any given point in time, if everyone wanted their money back, that money doesn't exist.

What Happens When You Factor in Taxes?

Tim was wearing away my skepticism on the above issues. But I had more concerns...

Me: "I can see how different mutual companies are from standard insurance companies. I can also see how they have been able to guarantee and deliver a 4% return for so many years. And how their history of dividends would get that 4% return up towards 5% or more.

"But what about taxes on those returns? How does that work?"

Tim: "Income for Life offers a combination of tax-deferred and tax-free growth. Policyholders are not required to report their policies, their dividends, or their interest to the IRS.

"Your dividends are always tax-free, no matter what. You'll never pay taxes on those.

"And once you want to start withdrawing additional money, you can take out what you paid in, tax-free.

"Let's say you paid $10,000 per year into a policy for 30 years. You'd be able to take out $300,000, completely tax-free.

"Why are dividends and what you paid in never taxed? It's because the IRS views withdrawing the money you paid in and the dividends you received as a return of your premium payments. It doesn't view life insurance dividends the same way as regular stock dividends. (I won't get into the technicalities of that here. For now, just know that the IRS doesn't tax life insurance dividends.)

"If you then wanted to withdraw more from your policy (factoring in the appreciation) than what you paid in, you'd have to start paying taxes on those withdrawals. Meanwhile, that money would have been growing tax-deferred.

"But... with the Income for Life strategy, there is a way to change the tax-deferred portion of your money to tax-free."

Me: "That doesn't sound legal. It makes me uncomfortable."

Tim: "It's perfectly legal. It's all about understanding the IRS rules and how they view things. There are no taxes owed on money you pull out up to your cost basis (what you paid in). If you kept withdrawing cash after your cost basis, you'd have to pay taxes. But instead of taking withdrawals from that point on, *you can start taking policy loans.*

"Let's say you've accumulated $1 million in cash value. And then, let's say you need to take out $30,000 each year for whatever reason. In the first 10 years, you take a straight withdrawal. You pull out $300,000 tax-free. That's your cost basis (what you paid in).

"Now, in year 11 and beyond, you take that $30,000 amount in the form of a loan from the insurance company.

"It's like income in that you still have $30,000 in your bank account each year to spend however you want, but the IRS won't tax you in year 11 and beyond. Why? *Because you're taking a loan from the insurance company, not a withdrawal from your policy.*

"And here's the trick: It is a loan you never intend to pay back.

"Getting back to our example: Let's say you take a $30,000 loan each year for 20 years. You'd have $600,000 in outstanding loans. You don't need to worry about that, though, because it will be settled by the insurance company.

"For example, if you have a $1.5 million death benefit in your policy, they'll keep $600,000 of that when you die to pay off the loan. Then they'll give the remaining amount of $900,000 to your estate."

Me: "So you *are* paying the taxes. You are paying them with your death benefit."

Tim: "No, you're just paying off the policy loan you have with the insurance company. The rest of the proceeds—$900,000—are tax-free. (Death benefit proceeds are always free of income tax.)

"Think of it this way. These life insurance policies can act like a Roth IRA, but with two additional benefits. There are no limits... and you have that 4% guarantee. You can't get that with an IRA."

> A Roth IRA lets you put after-tax money into an account and then never have to pay taxes on it again. In essence, you pay your taxes up front. You can then grow your money for decades. Roth IRAs are great, but there are major limitations. For instance, you can only put $5,500 per year into them. And if you make over $191,000 per year as a married couple filing jointly (or $120,000 as a single person), you can't contribute to them.

And What About Agents' Commissions?

Me: "I used to get 6.5% from municipal bonds. But they dropped to 4.5% in the mid-2000s. If I were to buy new munis today, I'd get maybe 2.5% for shorter-term bonds and maybe 4% for long-term bonds. I asked Dominick, my broker, if there were any other investments out there giving a guaranteed 4% return. He said, 'No, Mark, there are no guarantees... not even treasuries.'

"So that 4% guarantee is impressive.

"But let's talk about my big problem with whole-life policies: The agents' commissions are huge. On a single-premium policy, for example, they can range from 50-100%."

Tim: "This is the most common objection we get from people who understand how traditional whole-life insurance works. The commissions can be crazy high—as much 100% of the first-year premium. But that is when the policies are set up the traditional mainstream way... not the Income for Life way.

"Traditional whole-life policies are set up to provide policyholders with as much death benefit as possible. And since the agent's commission can be as high as 100% of that first-year payment, you end up with $0 in cash value the first year and very little in years two and three.

"But there's something called a paid-up additions rider. And it changes everything.

"Using this rider the way we recommend minimizes the death benefit to the lowest level possible. It also slashes the agent's commission up to 70%.

"So instead of 100% of the first premium payment going to the agent's commission, only 30-40% does.

"Lower death benefit focus means lower commissions. But you can't lower the fees any more than that. If you did, the IRS would look at your policy and say 'That's not life insurance. You're just using it to avoid paying taxes.'

"Getting the fees down to 30-40% of the first year payment is the lowest legal limit before you lose the tax-deferred growth benefits.

"So between having a lower death benefit and paying a much lower commission, the cash value in the policy is positive in year one and mounts quickly after that."

Me: "Fine. But I can't tolerate the idea of paying an insurance agent 30% of the first-year premium payment. That sounds outrageous. I pay Dominick, who does a great job handling my stock accounts, 1%. What's wrong with that?"

Tim: "Mark, life insurance commissions have by far the most misunderstood of any fee structure there is. It's because consumers don't have access to the commission schedules. And they latch on to the seemingly bad first-year commission, assuming it's the worst deal.

"But because I'm licensed, I have access to the schedules. I got licensed precisely for this reason... so I could study the schedules and really understand them.

"I have spent 50-plus hours building spreadsheets to find out for myself if life insurance fees were a rip-off.

"I used data from Tom's last policy, as well as its associated fee structure. And I was surprised to learn that the fee structure with life insurance is—in fact—the fairest and cheapest amongst investment products... even with that high first-year fee.

"Tom and I wrote an essay about it.

"Let me quickly recap the findings for you...

"In short, we took the money Tom would have paid into his policy over a 30-year period and put it into a mutual fund. A bond-type of mutual fund to mimic the same type of safety and returns. We screened Morningstar's database of thousands of bond funds and found the average expense fee to be 1%.

"Here's where things get interesting. With the same amount of money going in and at the same growth rate, we let each respective fee structure play out.

"Look at the chart below. The black line represents the total amount of Tom's life insurance fees in any given year. You can see that big spike in the first year for the insurance fees. Fund fees are much lower.

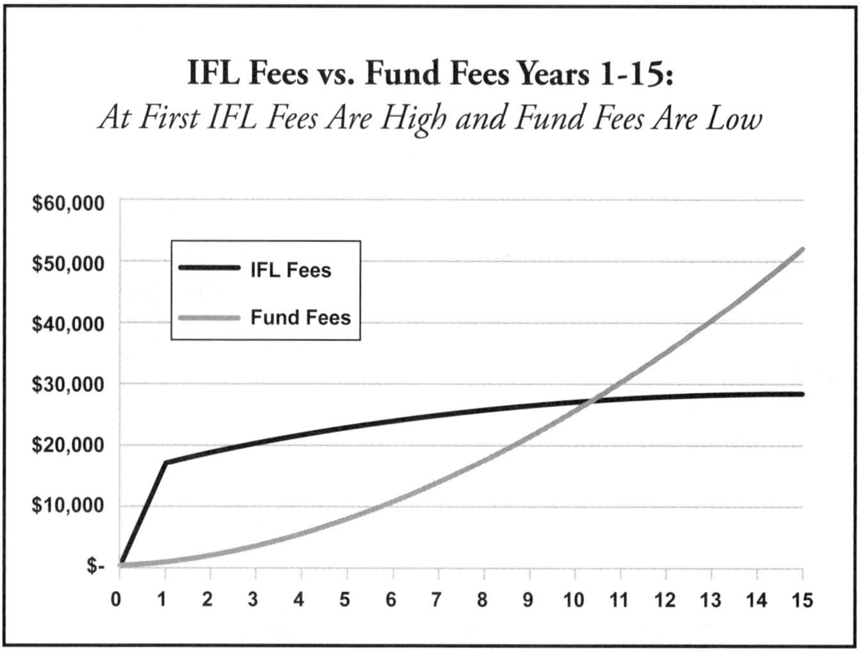

"In years 1-10, Tom would pay more in total fees with life insurance set up the Income for Life way. But in the 11th year, he would have more total fees with the mutual fund. From that point on, the fees grow exponentially higher with the mutual fund.

"How high? Let's fast-forward 50 years to when Tom is in his mid-80s.

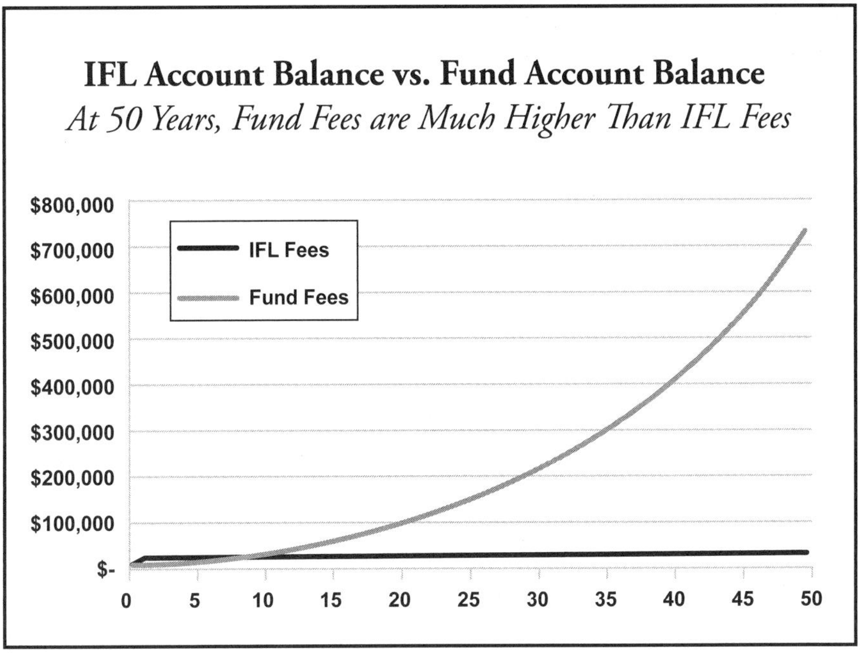

"How much would he have paid in total fees over 50 years in the bond mutual fund?

"$727,311.

"That's more than 20 times the $34,319 he'd end up paying in life insurance fees over the same period.

"With funds, your fee is based on the total amount of money under management. That 1% doesn't sound bad. And it isn't... at first. But as your account balance grows, so do the fees you pay.

"With life insurance, the insurance company bases its fees on the money you put into the policy each year—not on the account's total value.

"Think about it. In Tom's 30th year, he'll make a premium payment for $17,500 into his policy, and he'll pay a $175 fee. (After the first year, there are some small fees on the premium payments made. In this case, those fees are 1%.)

"If he were putting that $17,500 into his bond mutual fund in that 30th year, the 1% fee wouldn't be on his payment... but on *his entire account balance* of $1.48 million. And 1% of that is $14,877.

"So both have a 1% fee in the 30th year. But two very different results in the amount of fees paid.

"Look at the result of the mutual fund fee structure at year 50.

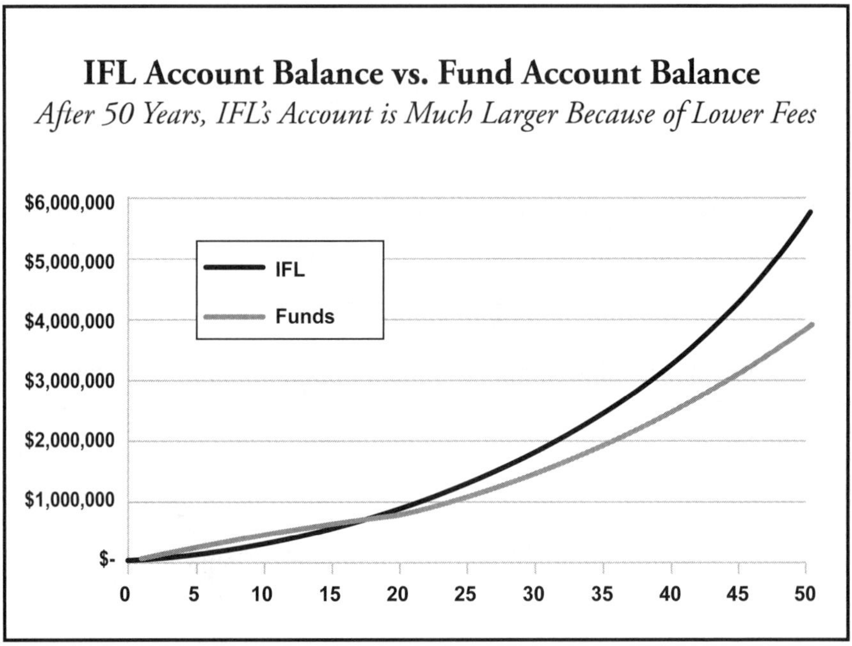

"That 1% mutual fund fee caused a difference of more than $1.8 million in final account value."

Me: "I have to admit that I never fully comprehended the total cost of those 1% fund fees.

"But what if I didn't use a managed account? How does the cost of Income for Life compare to a self-managed IRA?"

Tim: "Yes... that's the big argument. What if you manage and grow the money yourself. No fees (except a few brokerage commissions here and there).

"Well, now we're talking apples and oranges. With a self-managed IRA, you need to monitor, watch, rebalance, and stay disciplined with it over multiple decades. With Income for Life, you make one payment each year and let the most sophisticated money managers on the planet do all that managing for you.

"At the Palm Beach Research Group, we're all about educating and empowering investors to grow and manage their own money. To keep it out of Wall Street's reach.

"So if you think you can do better managing your account on your own, go for it. But I do know all too well that investors—as a group—underperform the market... by a wide margin.

"They buy stocks high. Then panic in a crash and sell them low. They set stop losses, but then ignore them and buy more when a stock gets cheaper. They ignore proper position sizing rules and put way too much into a single stock that blows up.

"Dalbar, a research firm, conducts studies each year on how individuals perform with their accounts. They confirm this—that investors perform a lot worse than the markets. In fact, they found that over the last 30 years, the average U.S. stock investor has underperformed the market by between three and seven percentage points per year. (The difference in the range depends on how the underperformance is calculated.)"

Me: "Yes. I'm familiar with such studies. And I can certainly see the advantage of having at least a portion of my investments set aside in this kind of policy where I can count on getting a 4-5% return.

"But now tell me more about the benefit of being able to borrow from your own Income for Life policy."

Becoming Your Own Bank

Tim: "That is a great benefit. My insurance company is willing to give me a loan for up to the amount I have in cash value. They'll do it anytime, no questions asked. And I'll have a check in three to five business days."

Me: "That's really convenient. But there are other ways to get the same convenience. If you maintain a significant cash balance with your bank, they will likely give you a line of credit. Or if you have municipal bonds with a broker, he'll lend you money against them.

"What are the typical borrowing costs?"

Tim: "The companies we are recommending to *Palm Beach Letter* readers offer rates between 4.5% and 6%. (Some others charge as much as 8.5%.)"

Me: "I can borrow money much more cheaply than that—and, in fact, I am doing it with two lines of credit I've opened for business purposes. One is with Bank of America at 3.1%. The other is with Raymond James for 1.7%."

Tim: "Yes, but that's because you pledge those credit lines against assets you have with those institutions."

Me: "You're right about my credit line with Raymond James. It's backed by my bond account. And I can't withdrawal that collateral without collapsing the line of credit.

"But my credit line with Bank of America is not collateralized. It's based on my history of keeping a large cash balance—which, in all fairness, isn't true for most people.

"And how is that any different from what you do? You can borrow only up to the cash value of your account. Isn't that the same thing?"

Tim: "It's almost the same thing. Borrowing against the cash in my policy allows me to double-compound my money. My money continues to grow in the policy. And the insurance company loans me money that I can use to invest.

"You've found a way to do the same thing. You invest in bonds. And you've established a line of credit against those bonds. You can borrow from your broker and invest. Your rates are great.

"But let me ask you a few questions...

"Even though you have a broker, don't you still have to oversee your bond account? You don't have to do that with the policy.

"Is your bond portfolio safe against lawsuits or creditor claims? In most states, it's virtually impossible for anyone to get to your life insurance policy.

"And does your bond portfolio have a death benefit? That's the biggest missing piece to me. The death benefit is not the primary reason we're setting up these policies. But it's a phenomenal perk that can give the average person more retirement income options later in life.

"So, yes, you are effectively doing the same thing. You can borrow against your bonds and invest the money to 'double compound.' And you have a cheap cost of capital. But I'd wager most of our readers can't get the same terms... or don't have multimillion-dollar bond portfolios like you do, Mark. And your bonds don't come with a death benefit."

Me: "So let's see...

"Your cost of money at 4.7% is much higher—nearly 176%—than my 1.7% Raymond James line of credit.

"Like Income for Life, my municipal bonds provide guaranteed returns (if the state or municipality doesn't go under). And these are not just tax-deferred—they are tax-free. My current portfolio, for example, is giving me an average yield of 4.5%, according to my broker, Dominick. But that amounts to 7.5% since I'm in the top tax bracket.

"And Dominick doesn't charge me an annual fee to manage my bonds. Just a 1% fee when I buy them. (Admittedly, that's because I'm a client with a larger-than-normal account.)

"Lower management fees. A higher rate of return. And lower borrowing costs. So why wouldn't a municipal bond account, even at today's crummy rates of only 1.75% for 10 years, 2.65% for 20 years, and 2.8% for 30 years be better than Income for Life?"

Tim: "If you're strictly looking at investment and rate of return performance, sure. With an Income for Life policy, you start in the hole because of that first year fee. And so, of course, you'd do better investing in something else.

"But this is taking a very narrow view. Over time, the returns in a policy get better.

"And besides, Tom and I aren't saying to put all your money into Income for Life. It's not a decision between all Income for Life or all bonds. Or all Income for Life or all Legacy.

"Why not do a bit of both?"

Me: "I was already coming to that same conclusion myself."

Tim: "No other investment vehicle on the planet can offer as much safety, as many guarantees, and the same versatility as dividend-paying whole-life insurance from a mutual insurance company.

"And, again... as for the borrowing costs against a muni-bond portfolio? You have very privileged rates because of how much money you have. The majority of our readers are not in that position.

"Besides, did you know your broker or bank can take away your lines of credit whenever they want to? It happened during the financial crisis of 2008. Dozens of banks and brokerages retracted outstanding lines of credit with even their best customers. It screwed over many small-business owners who relied on those lines of credits to run their businesses."

Me: "I hadn't thought of that."

Tim: "With a dividend-paying whole-life insurance policy from a mutual company like the ones we recommend, the policy loan feature is a contractual guarantee. It's built right into the language of the policy contract. You can request a loan anytime, no questions asked.

"There are plenty of examples throughout history of entrepreneurs who turned to their policies for loans when banks turned them down. J. C. Penney used a loan from his policy to help meet payroll in the late-1920s after the stock market crashed.

"In 1953, Walt Disney couldn't get a bank to lend him money to start Disneyland. So he turned to the only place that would, his insurance company, for a policy loan.

"You can't downplay or ignore the guaranteed nature of the returns and access to your money via a policy loan... even in the worst of times.

"Tom and I prefer to store our cash in our policies. Then, when we need it or when we see a compelling investment opportunity, we can quickly access the cash.

"When, for example, a rental property comes up that my real estate investment group is interested in, I tap my policy. I call up the insurance company and borrow money for my portion of the down payment. I have the money three days later.

"Because I'm using the insurance company's money, the money in my policy still grows. I'm just using the money I have as collateral. Just like you are with your bond portfolio and your lines of credit."

Me: "Okay, I must say, it sounds pretty good. Especially for people like you guys—who are relatively young and don't have assets you can use as collateral."

"But I have two more concerns. And they are *not* minor.

The Caveat

"If I understand it correctly, when you open an Income for Life policy, the idea is that you must continue to make premiums for the rest of your life. Is that true?"

Tim: "Yes. And this is important. You really shouldn't open a policy if you don't plan to keep it in force for your lifetime."

Me: "Why is that?"

Tim: "There are two reasons...

"First, because of the initially higher commission in the first year, you will lose money if you cancel the policy after just a few years. It takes a while—usually four to seven years—before the cash balance in your policy equals the premium payments you've paid in.

"Second, because the whole idea of the account is to take advantage of tax-deferred saving on a long-term basis. With each year that passes, the strategy becomes more efficient. Dividends get higher and the cash value increases.

"That's why we are very clear in explaining that you should never cancel an Income for Life policy. And there is no reason to. Because if you ever need money—for whatever reason—you can get it by taking out a loan. (Remember, the loan is backed by the cash value in your policy.)"

Me: "But having to pay into the policy every year for the rest of your life—that is onerous, isn't it?"

Tim: "Actually, Mark, it's not. Eventually, there is enough cash and dividends in the account to cover all future premium payments. At that point, the policy basically covers itself.

"The insurance jargon for that is 'automatic premium offset.' But Tom and I prefer to describe it as 'putting your policy on autopilot.'"

Me: "How long does it take to get to that point?"

Tim: "If you start off with a large first-year premium payment, it's possible to have the account go on autopilot in year three. But for a lot of our readers, it will take considerably longer—between five and 10 years.

"Tom's latest policy could go on autopilot after he makes his fourth premium payment. But, of course, he'll keep paying in because he wants to store cash there. Still, it's a good option to have."

Knowledge by Logic and Knowledge from Experience

Me: "It all makes sense to me intellectually. But I have one final concern. For me, this is theoretical knowledge. I don't have any actual experience with whole-life insurance. And I can't recommend it to our readers until I do.

"I promise that I'll open up an Income for Life account and see what happens."

Tim: "Mark, you already have a whole-life policy. Didn't you tell me that Agora (Palm beach Research Group's holding company) took out a 'key man' life insurance policy on you about four years ago?"

Me: "Yes."

Tim: "Well, that's a type of whole-life insurance.

"Look into it. And when you get the information, we'll get together and I'll help you interpret it."

Here's What I Found Out...

Agora started this policy for me in 2010. It apparently shut down an older policy it had for me and used the proceeds to fund this new one.

The premium payments on this policy are $60,000 per year. But my old policy had $630,519 cash in it. Agora transferred that into the policy as the first-year payment. (That's known as a 1035 Exchange—a tax-free transfer of funds from one policy to another.)

Using the numbers I had, Tim put together the following chart—a 20-year snapshot to show me how the policy has (and should) performed.

Date	Year	Age	Premium Payment	Total Paid	Cash Value	Death Benefit	Total Return
2010	1	60	$690,519	$690,519	$650,255	$2,060,949	(5.83)%
2011	2	61	$60,000	$750,519	$730,907	$2,060,949	(1.37)%
2012	3	62	$60,000	$810,519	$822,660	$2,060,949	0.54%
2013	4	63	$60,000	$870,519	$919,318	$2,060,949	1.53%
2014	5	64	$60,000	$930,519	$1,002,084	$2,060,949	1.71%
2015	6	65	$60,000	$990,519	$1,102,486	$2,060,949	2.11%
2016	7	66	--	$990,519	$1,147,441	$2,060,949	2.43%
2017	8	67	--	$990,519	$1,193,945	$2,060,949	2.66%
2018	9	68	--	$990,519	$1,242,039	$2,060,949	2.82%
2019	10	69	--	$990,519	$1,291,754	$2,060,949	2.95%
2020	11	70	--	$990,519	$1,348,535	$2,060,949	3.09%
2021	12	71	--	$990,519	$1,407,466	$2,060,949	3.21%
2022	13	72	--	$990,519	$1,468,953	$2,108,091	3.30%
2023	14	73	--	$990,519	$1,532,278	$2,159,498	3.38%
2024	15	74	--	$990,519	$1,597,484	$2,212,043	3.44%
2025	16	75	--	$990,519	$1,664,571	$2,265,440	3.49%
2026	17	76	--	$990,519	$1,733,464	$2,319,835	3.53%
2027	18	77	--	$990,519	$1,804,038	$2,374,976	3.56%
2028	19	78	--	$990,519	$1,876,245	$2,431,047	3.59%
2029	20	79	--	$990,519	$1,949,649	$2,487,855	3.60%

And here's how he explained it to me:

1. My Break-even Point

"In the first year," Tim told me, "you paid $690,519... but your cash value is $650,255. You're in the hole. That's why the return column on the far right is negative. It's because of that first-year fee. More on that in a minute.

"Notice that after your third premium payment, you've paid in a total of $810,519 and your cash balance is now $822,660. That third year is when you break even based on what you've paid in.

2. My ROI or Return

"Now look at that last column. That is what represents your total return. It's what you'd have to earn in a separate account each and every year to end up with the cash value balance in the policy.

"So let's look at year five. It's saying your return is 1.71%. That's basically saying if you were to invest those five years of premium payments elsewhere, you'd have to earn 1.71% each year for five years in a row to end up with the $1,002,084 cash value that's in your policy.

"You can see my point that these policies are not that exciting right away. They grow slowly at first. Fast-forward to the 20th year. That's where the returns for your policy top out.

"At that point, it would be the equivalent of earning 3.6% on that cash each year for 20 years in a row.

"The natural objection at this point is—where is the total 5% return I've been talking about?

"It's important for readers to know that the returns are not cookie-cutter. They depend on several factors, including your age, sex, and health rating.

"Returns on policies for older people, for example, aren't as great as they are for younger people. There is a higher likelihood that an older person will pass away sooner. And in your case, they issued you a mediocre health rating because you smoke cigars. The insurance companies take this into account."

3. Commissions and Fees

"Mark, your agent on this told you that his first year commission was $37,146. We can't include that against the $630,000 that was transferred in. So that $37,146 represented about 62% of your first year $60,000 premium payment.

"That's a little higher than the 30-40% of your first year premium payment I was talking about. My guess is that he made a separate small fee on the transfer of the existing amount."

4. My Autopilot Point

"Did you notice that after the sixth premium payment next year, there aren't any more premiums due?

"When Agora set this policy up, it had a $60,000 premium payment each year for your life. But it looks like it's elected to put the policy on autopilot after making next year's sixth premium payment.

"That means there is now enough cash and dividends in the policy to make all future premium payments. And look at the cash value column—it continues to grow each year even though you're not paying into it."

In Summary

This has been a long, detailed chapter, so I'll make my conclusion short.

I believe the Income for Life program is a good to very good addition to most wealth-building plans. Its primary benefit—the 5% (4% guaranteed, plus 1% in dividends) compounded, tax-free return—is very difficult, if not impossible, to replicate. I also like the loan feature for people who don't have large bond portfolios. My endorsement is based on both the knowledge I've acquired from my many discussions with Tim and Tom and on my own personal experience, being four years into a whole-life insurance program through Agora.

It's a particularly attractive policy for young people, who have so many years of appreciation ahead of them. But it can also work for middle-aged people who want to leave money for their children or for charity.

I would not recommend committing as much to the program as Tom and Tim are personally doing. If you like the idea of Income for Life, I'd begin conservatively, allocating a portion of your investible income and/or investible net worth to it. Then increase it, if you want, later on.

PART 5:

Pressing the "Start" Button

CHAPTER 13

The Hidden Feature You Need to Know About Before Starting

Income for Life has numerous benefits, including the fact that it's private, grows tax-free, is untouchable by lawsuits, and compounds money four or five times faster than any other savings vehicle in existence.

But there's one benefit we haven't talked much about yet. Mark and Tim hinted at it in the last chapter.

This benefit could be the biggest of them all.

I'm talking about using a special feature that comes with a dividend-paying whole-life insurance policy (the kind we use with Income for Life).

It's called the policy loan. And you can use it to cover any large expense, such as a vacation to Europe. Or college tuition fees for your children. Or medical bills.

I'm also talking about using this Income for Life policy loan feature to invest in the stock market, options, gold, bonds, or fine art.

You can even use it to start your own small business.

In short, Income for Life is like having your own bank or line of credit. Using the cash in your policy as collateral, you can borrow money from the insurance company any time you want.

Collateral is when you pledge a valuable asset in exchange for receiving a loan. For example, if you want a loan from a bank to invest in a risky start up business, that bank will ask for collateral before loaning you money. If the business venture fails and you can't pay back your loan, the bank can take your collateral as recourse.

You can spend this money however you like. And you can pay yourself back whenever—or however—you want.

Once you save enough cash in your policy, you'll never have to pay interest to another credit card, bank, or credit union again.

What else will you get from using this policy loan feature?

- No more credit checks
- No more loan applications
- No more rigid payback terms
- No more stressing about your credit score.

Think about how much money the average person "throws away" by paying interest and fees to banks, credit card companies, and other financing businesses. Now think about having the ability to use your Income for Life policy as your own bank—it's a benefit that could easily be worth several million dollars over the course of a lifetime.

Borrowing money from your policy is the easiest way in existence to borrow money.

Loan Approval in Less Than Five Minutes

Applying for a traditional bank loan is a major hassle.

Here are some of the things you'll need to do to get a loan in America today:

- Fill out a long application form
- Permit a close analysis of your credit report and score
- Have held a steady job for a minimum of two years
- Have a certain income level

- Have a certain amount of assets
- Provide proof of employment, income, and assets with documentation such as pay stubs and tax returns
- Make sure you have few other debts
- Pay loan origination and broker fees
- Sign mountains of paperwork.

After all this hassle, there's no guarantee your bank will even approve you for the loan.

But what if there were a better, easier, smoother way to borrow money?

Dividend-paying whole-life insurance policies come with guaranteed loan provisions. In simple language, this means that the insurance company has a legal obligation to lend you money whenever you want.

You won't be asked any questions. And you won't go through any loan application process.

The insurance company is willing to do this because it holds your money, so it's not taking any risk by lending to you.

The catch is that you can borrow only as much as you've saved up in your Income for Life policy (that's known as the "cash value"). For example, if you have $20,000 in cash value, you can get a loan from the insurance company for up to $20,000.

So what are the advantages of borrowing money from a mutual insurance company over a traditional bank? There are many. But today, I want to tell you about four of them.

Advantage No. 1—Guaranteed Loans

If you have $20,000 saved in your Income for Life policy, you can borrow $20,000 from the mutual insurance company—no questions asked. The insurance company can't refuse your request for a loan. As part-owner of the mutual insurance company, you're given this perk with your policy.

Imagine how powerful this is.

When would you need money most? It could be when you just lost a job and are in transition to find another one. Or your business could need a small infusion of cash to get through some temporary setbacks.

When you apply for a loan from a traditional bank, there are no guarantees the bank will approve you. If you've just lost your job and have no income... forget it. Your loan officer will never approve your loan.

If your business is struggling, your loan officer may decline you access to new money or a line of credit because of your hard times. (By the way, this happened to thousands of business owners in the financial crisis of 2008-2009.)

With traditional banks, you are at the mercy of their ever-changing rules and the changing economic environment.

Advantage No. 2—No Applications or Credit Checks

When I first opened my Income for Life policies, I was starting a renovation project. I planned to get a loan from a bank to pay for it. But I knew my policy had enough cash for this project, and I wanted to test the loan process to see for myself.

I picked up the phone and told the customer service representative I wanted to take out a policy loan. She asked me for my policy number and then asked how much I wanted.

She punched away on her keyboard for a couple minutes and then ended by saying, "You'll get a check in three business days." Sure enough, it showed up in my mailbox at the end of the week.

I couldn't believe it.

Now, if I had taken out this loan from a traditional bank, I—likely—would have had to set aside a couple of hours one afternoon to fill out all of the paperwork and gather all of the documentation for the loan officer. Then I'd wait another week for all of the papers to shuffle around to each person involved before I got the money.

Advantage No. 3—Setting Your Own Terms

With a loan from a mutual insurance company against your policy, you're in full control. You set the terms of repayment.

The insurance company will charge you a minimum amount of interest for the loan. As I write, rates are between 4.5% and 5%. Some mutual companies charge higher rates—up to 8%.

Want to set up a seven-year, rather than a five-year, payback schedule on your loan so your payments are lower? Go for it.

Do you want to pay off your loan over 10 years? No problem.

Or what if, midterm, you want to change your payback schedule from a five-year payback to a 10-year payback?

Or what if you wanted to make payments quarterly or semi-annually?

Again, no problem.

Once you've funded your policy long enough, you could also have the option to never pay back the loan if you don't want to. And the beautiful thing is that the insurance company couldn't care less.

How can that be?

If you don't pay back your loan, the insurance company will just keep track of the interest you owe.

It knows you're going to die someday. And when you do, it'll just pay off the loan and accrued interest with the proceeds of your family's death benefit check.

Advantage No. 4—Flexibility

What happens if you have a car loan from a bank and you start missing payments? First, your credit score will take a hit. Once you miss enough payments, your bank will send the local towing company for a midnight visit to seize your car.

What happens if you start missing your mortgage payments? The same thing. Your credit score takes a hit. You'll start getting letters from the bank. Eventually, the bank will foreclose on your house and send the local sheriff to kick you out.

With a loan from your mutual insurance company, you've got plenty of flexibility for unknown events life might throw at you.

Need a couple of months' break from loan payments because you lost your job or just had a big, unexpected expense? No problem. You won't have to worry about damaging your credit score. Or the bank repossessing your car.

Of course, missing payments is not a good habit to get into. But it sure is a nice option to have if you need it.

In short, the policy loan feature that comes with Income for Life policies offers a powerful, unique, and unmatched alternative to the traditional financing process with banks.

If you've dealt with a traditional bank, you know that these four perks I mentioned are a big deal.

You can use your policy like a bank, including using it to pay expenses, take vacations, invest, and start your own business.

The uses and possibilities are endless.

With enough commitment to funding an Income for Life policy, you can work toward eliminating traditional banks from your life for good.

And with enough commitment to learning about the different strategies available, you'll be able to use Income for Life to help you create a fortune.

CHAPTER 14

The Quickest Way to Begin Income for Life

In 2011, the Palm Beach Research Group hired a life insurance investigator.

We paid him to investigate the Income for Life industry and figure out which Income for Life experts we could recommend to you, if any.

> *"Not only should our experts have the experience," I said, "but they should also have perfect reputations. And, most important of all, they must use the Income for Life strategy with their own money."*

This investigator was already familiar with the industry. Plus, he'd read all of the books on Income for Life, he'd attended both major Income for Life conferences, he knew more than a dozen of the top Income for Life experts, and he'd spoken with dozens of Income for Life customers.

He'd also taken out several of his own Income for Life policies on himself and his family members.

You've heard me mention him a few times already in this book.

Our investigator's name is Tim Mittelstaedt. He did such a thorough investigation that I hired Tim to work for Palm Beach Research Group full time. And he's now our director of new product development.

Tim and I chose the best Income for Life agency to help serve our readers. It has hundreds of clients. Its agents have set up thousands of Income for Life policies. And these agents have more than 53 years of combined experience in this industry.

Most importantly, they all put their own money… lots of it… into Income for Life policies.

We know them, we like them, and we trust them. And we recommend them to Palm Beach Research Group readers because they understand how to set up and use our Income for Life strategy better than anyone else. It's as simple as that.

If you're already a subscriber to *The Palm Beach Letter* (one of the flagship publications at the Palm Beach Research Group), you'll know whom to call. You'll be able to find the contact information from our preferred group near the bottom of our special report:

http://palmbeachgroup.com/how-to-fund-your-own-worry-free-100-tax-free-retirement/

Note: If you're not a *Palm Beach Letter* subscriber, visit www.palmbeachletter1.com to learn how you can become one and get access to our preferred Income for Life expert.

Now, you might be tempted to go about this on your own… to find your own agent or use a family friend.

Please, I need to ask you to be aware: 95% of the information online about Income for Life is published by opportunistic life insurance salespeople using the movement to generate sales for their own life insurance businesses.

These scammers post free information online (sometimes using Income for Life terminology) and try to convert the traffic Google sends their way.

The Income for Life strategy is very specific. If you don't set it up right, it won't work as well. You'll waste thousands of dollars and end up with a horrible mess.

Some of these agents might be good guys, and they might mean well. They understand the Income for Life concept and they'll take good care of you.

But we can't know for certain.

Most of these agents are bad guys. They don't understand Income for Life at all. They'll sell you a garbage insurance product that's not compatible with this strategy, and give they'll you terrible service. Or worse, they'll set up your policy and then disappear. Later in life, when you have questions or want to use your policy, they're nowhere to be found.

We know of several Palm Beach Research Group readers who've been duped this way.

So why take the risk?

This is your livelihood we're talking about. And your retirement. Don't throw it away by working with an unqualified agent. Better to sleep well at night knowing your policy was set up correctly by an agency that'll be there for you for the rest of your life.

FURTHER RESOURCES

Income for Life is a great place to save money and earn up to 5% on your cash over the long term. But once you open and fund an Income for Life policy, there are dozens of strategies you can do to generate more wealth and save money using the policy loan feature.

If you're interested in learning more, we cover these advanced wealth-building strategies in our Income for Life *Premium* service.

In this program, I take you through all the advanced techniques my team and I are using to safely build our own wealth that we can enjoy now...

That's where we cover how to pay down debt, cover unexpected medical expenses, and even how to invest in real estate (and many other "tricks")—all using Income for Life.

We call these techniques "advanced," but they aren't complicated. You just need someone to explain them to you for the first time. That's exactly what we have done with this interactive product—take you step by step through all of these strategies that you can use to create massive wealth more quickly.

For example, over your lifetime, did you know you can save up to $250,000 by purchasing cars with Income for Life?

Or that you can use Income for Life to boost retirement income up to 50%.

But the best part is... you can "turbocharge" the 5% these policies pay over time, thanks to a strategy we call "Dual Compounding."

Instead of compounding your savings in one place—your Income for Life account where you're earning a safe 5%—you're compounding the same money in two places at the same time... and getting much bigger returns (5% from the insurance company, plus an additional 12-32% on top).

One subscriber (who wishes to be identified as "R.C.") wrote in and said, "Since I've been doing this, just over three years now, I have averaged 32% per year... I don't really stress over finances anymore."

"Dual Compounding" may be the greatest wealth secret we've ever discovered at the Palm Beach Research Group.

We cover exactly how to use "Dual Compounding" and more in our Income for Life *Premium* service.

Since you have already read this book and are interested in the Income for Life strategy, we have arranged a special offer just for you. Call 888-501-2598 to find out more, or you can watch the video found at www.incomeforlifeoffer.com, which also gives detailed information on the website and strategies we provide with this unique service.